“WHEN I GO BACK TO MY HOME COUNTRY”

"WHEN I GO BACK TO MY HOME COUNTRY"

:

a Remembrance *of* Archie Ammons

by

EMILY HERRING WILSON

R.A. FOUNTAIN
FOUNTAIN, NC

Books by Emily Herring Wilson

Nonfiction

"When I Go Back to My Home Country": a Remembrance of Archie Ammons 2019

The Three Graces of Val-Kill: Eleanor Roosevelt, Marion Dickerman, and Nancy Cook in the Place They Made Their Own 2017

North Carolina Women: Making History (with Margaret Supplee Smith) 1999

No One Gardens Alone: A Life of Elizabeth Lawrence 2004

Get a Good Life 1997

For the People of North Carolina: The Z. Smith Reynolds Foundation at Half-century, 1936–1986 1988

Hope and Dignity: Older Black Women of the South 1983

Poetry

To Fly without Hurry 2001

Arise Up and Call Her Blessed 1982

Solomon's Seal 1978

Balancing on Stones 1975

Down Zion's Alley 1972

Edited by Emily Herring Wilson

Becoming Elizabeth Lawrence: Discovered Letters of a Southern Gardener 2010

Two Gardeners: Katharine S. White and Elizabeth Lawrence—A Friendship in Letters 2002

This remembrance is dedicated to John Ammons Eddie, Sally, and Julie Wilson

Archie peeks into Emily's office at Cornell.
photo by Emily Herring Wilson, 1993

Printed in the United States of America

Grateful acknowledgement is made to the following publications in which these poems originally appeared:
"Still," *The Emerson Review*; "For Emily Wilson, from a Newcomer," *Chelsea*; "For Emily Wilson," "For Edwin Wilson," and "Easter Morning," *Poetry*; "I Was Born in," *The Mule Poems* by A.R. Ammons; "I Went Back " and "Keeping Track," *North Carolina Literary Review*; "Chiseled Clouds," *Epoch*; "My Father, I Hollow for You," *The Iowa Review*; "Between Each Song," *American Poetry Review*; "Nelly Myers," "Father," and "Corsons Inlet," *Hudson Review*; and "Chinaberry," *The Quest*.

Grateful acknowledgement is made to John R. Ammons for permission to reprint two prose pieces by A.R. Ammons, "Ten Years Ago I Was," originally published in *An Image for Longing: Selected Letters and Journals of A.R. Ammons 1951–1974*, by the University of Victoria, and "[Prose statement on painting]" originally published in *Changing Things*, by Palemon Press; and the poem "I Was Born in." Copyright John R. Ammons.

Cover photo at Critz, VA, 1980, and photo on page 2, Reynolda House, 1981, by Susan Mullally

Printed by Morgan Printers, Greenville, NC on a Heidelberg PM74 offset press on Neenah Classic Crest paper composed in Mrs Eaves typeface designed by Zuzana Licko.

First edition

Design by Eva Roberts
Published by R.A Fountain, P.O. Box 44, Fountain, NC 27829-0044 USA

Library of Congress Cataloging-in-Publication Data
Wilson, Emily Herring.
"When I go back to my home country," a remembrance of Archie Ammons
Includes bibliographical sources, index, and timeline

ISBN 978-0-9842102-3-7 paperback

1. Ammons, A.R., 1926–2001. 2. Poets, American—twentieth century Biography. 3. Emily Herring Wilson, 1939–. 4. English teachers—United States Biography. 5. Southern writers. 6. Education, history—North Carolina. 7. Winston-Salem (N.C)—Wake Forest University. 8. Ithaca (N.Y.)—Cornell University.

TABLE OF CONTENTS

11	Prologue
15	A Homecoming, 1972
22	On Campus
26	"Still," a poem by A.R. Ammons
28	Hatteras, 1949–50
30	"Hairpin," a poem by Emily Herring Wilson
35	"Ten Years Ago I Was," by A.R. Ammons, 1950
36	A Sabbatical Question, 1973
38	Sabbatical, 1974–75, part 1
43	"For Emily Wilson, from a Newcomer," a poem by A.R. Ammons
45	A Day Trip Interrupted
46	Sabbatical, part 2
48	Interlude: Two Poems by A.R. Ammons "For Edwin Wilson" and "For Emily Wilson"
52	Sabbatical, part 3
58	*The Nickelodeon*
63	"The Bread and Butter of Life," a poem by Emily Herring Wilson
64	Day Trip to Old Wake Forest
71	"I Was Born in," a poem by A.R. Ammons
72	"My Home Country": Columbus County
76	Five Poems by A.R. Ammons: "I Went Back," "Chiseled Clouds," "Father," "Motioning," and "My Father, I Hollow for You"
81	Day Trip to Columbus County

83	"Beginning an Epic," a poem by Emily Herring Wilson
84	Sabbatical, part 4
88	Friends for Life
92	Ticks and Teeth
94	No
98	Wake Forest, 1986
100	More Friends
113	My Cornell Semester, 1993
123	Farewells
126	Vida Ammons Cox
131	Two Poems by A.R. Ammons "Keeping Track" and "Between Each Song"
134	An Email from Phyllis
138	Afterword
142	Timeline
150	Jackpine Press
151	Sources
153	Index

when I go back to my home country in these
fresh far-away days, it's convenient to visit
everybody, aunts and uncles, those who used to say,
look how he's shooting up, and the
trinket aunts who always had a little
something in their pocketbooks, cinnamon bark
or a penny or a nickel. . .

—*from* ***"Easter Morning"*** *by* A.R. AMMONS

Prologue

To have a poet for a friend changes the way I feel about poets. My first poet, like yours, I suspect, was Mother Goose. Whoever heard of such a person! And yet, I did believe that Mary could be quite contrary, and that a spider could frighten Miss Muffet away. In school the poets we read were people in books, in a far-away time and place. We were told, and we believed, that William Shakespeare was a genius. Emily Dickinson, a mystery. Walt Whitman, a wild man. Not normal people, for sure. And yet, the fascination I felt for their poems surpassed everything in my daily life—I could not explain, or wish to explain, the feeling of transport to another world, but a world of words matched somehow, many times, my own feelings. *I wandered lonely as a cloud.* Of course I did. Who knew I felt that way? And then in college, I met a living poet—Randall Jarrell—like an actor on a stage: handsomely bearded, with a beautiful wife and a sports car. Out of reach—no one like anyone I'd ever seen, but there he was, my teacher, writing a poem about a girl in the library. Poetry, however different, seemed to speak to me, and yet, why did I assume that these makers of poems were not like me?

And then it happened: I met Archie, said to be a famous poet, but who over almost thirty years would become more like a member of my family, a father or brother, a farmer, or preacher. Somebody I'd see at the K&W Cafeteria. A jokey man who made me laugh. An angry man who made me mad. Sometimes grumpy, sometimes kind. A friend who read to me what he wrote and read what I wrote. For I, in my ordinary way, was a poet, too.

This is my story of a friendship and my story of a poet, A.R. Ammons. Everybody called him Archie.

I begin at the end, for as T.S. Eliot said, "to make an end is to make a beginning."

: : :

At the end of our weekly telephone call, near the end of his life, Archie said, "I depend on you." These were not his last words to me—those would come months later on the day before he died, a week after his 75th birthday, February 25, 2001. But they were the words I wrote on a scrap of paper and have kept for sixteen years. Each year I would read them again and ponder the meaning. I had no way of knowing if others had been given the same message; after all, he had Cornell University colleagues who had known him over many years and critics who had written voluminously about his poetry. Certainly his literary reputation did not depend on me. My own writing career is modest, and I had no important contacts in the publishing world. He could be certain that I would always remain close to his family. What was my role? I believe that Archie realized he had never had a better friend. He thought I would know what to do.

When my husband, Ed Wilson, Provost at Wake Forest University, invited Archie to spend a sabbatical in North Carolina, Archie thought about the offer seriously. He was ten years into his career at Cornell, with nine collections of poetry in print, and an offer, also, to spend this year at Yale. When he and his wife, Phyllis, and their young son, John, decided to spend the 1974-75 academic year at Wake Forest, he renewed his bond to the state, to his sisters, and to Wake Forest, his undergraduate alma mater. It was a year, as Archie said, that changed the whole family. During the next thirty years, he returned to his home state many times, taking up short-term residences, attending celebrations in his honor, eating out at his favorite place—the K&W cafeteria—and visiting friends and family in eastern North Carolina. He and Phyllis discovered that they could live in the South. But over the years, the reasons that they couldn't grew: He felt himself growing old, as he told his readers. Perhaps he could not write anymore. He needed to save money to leave to his son; he had to keep up appearances (graciously accept his many prizes) as the holder of a distinguished Chair at Cornell; and his health would worsen (a heart attack in 1989, followed by triple by-pass surgery). It was too late to pull up stakes. Although he had enjoyed living in North Carolina—and would enjoy his many visits—he felt better staying where he was. He retired from Cornell in 1998 and spent the rest of his years in Ithaca.

: : :

In 2017, when *The Complete Poems of A.R. Ammons*, edited by Robert M. West, was published in two hefty volumes by Norton, I placed them on my desk and began to write my memories of Archie. I knew him well for more than three decades, and I suspect that I know as much about him as anyone. But I do not bring a critic's reading to his poems or an evaluation of where he ranks among the great poets. I do not practice psychology, I am not an intellectual, and I find many of his long poems incomprehensible and sometimes boring. But I am a lifelong Southerner, and I know his home country of North Carolina. He and I were proud of our heritage, faults and all. We depended upon—and defended—one another.

This is what I have to give in return for his many gifts to me: my love. I don't know if my memories will bring readers closer to welcoming a poet into their lives, which is my intention. But it is my true story to give, and I know that Phyllis, Archie, and their son, John, and Archie's sister Vida trusted my judgment. Once Archie said, "You understand me better than anyone." Phyllis agreed. Of course they were not thinking of the knowledge of a great literary critic—that place of honor belongs to Helen Vendler, our dear friend, and Harold Bloom. But Archie knew that I liked the ordinariness of what he called "the real world," and we both managed to thrive as outsiders (outspoken critics) and as insiders (members of the establishment) on university campuses, and we remained self-taught. Archie told me, "I never wanted to be a Poet Poet. I wanted to be an amateur poet." I am his amateur reader.

I thank many friends for encouraging me to write this book, especially three who always believed I should: Kenneth Frazelle, Rick Mashburn, and Ken McClane. I also thank Archie's and Phyllis's son, John Ammons, and Archie's sister Vida Ammons Cox, for whom this is written. Alex Albright at R.A. Fountain has been a thoughtful and generous editor and publisher.

Archie loved us all, for love was his deepest reserve, and he would say to each of us, "Thank you for coming along."

photo by Susan Mullally, Reynolda House, 1981

A Homecoming, May 1972

I had been darting around making anxious talk, on the sly studying the great poet, not his poems, but him—tall, balding, with a ruff of red hair at the edges; very fair skin, long, loose arms; big hands, baggy pants—when I noticed he had slipped away from the group and appeared to be leaving us. A.R. Ammons, here at Wake Forest to receive an honorary degree the next day at the 1972 commencement, had driven alone to Winston-Salem from Cornell in Ithaca, New York, leaving behind Phyllis and their son, John, to see his two sisters, Mona and Vida (and their families), who were still living in North Carolina, and to be ceremoniously feted by his school.

Archie had shown little interest in meeting anyone other than his family. Now the English faculty had gathered at the house of the department chair, Elizabeth Phillips, to show off the new campus of Wake Forest, which in 1956 had moved to Winston-Salem, in 1965 became a university, and in 1971 began admitting graduate students. Archie had been a student on the original campus in Wake County, where he had taken a freshman English class with Ed Wilson, the administrator who had invited him back to receive an honorary degree. Surprised to be remembered, Archie had accepted, with caution—for one, he said that he had felt "invisible" on the old campus as a student and preferred to remain so; and furthermore, he did not want to sit on the stage. Ed told him, that in reading poems in *The Hudson Review* by A.R. Ammons, he wondered if he could be the "Archie Ammons" in his English class at Wake Forest College, who sat "on the last row seat next to the aisle," and for whom "it was easy to put down an A for the course." Yes, he was the same Archie. The English Department was enthusiastic about claiming a prize-winning poet as one of their own. Moreover, he could establish any conditions that made him feel more comfortable, and Ed agreed with Archie's suggestion that he stand on the side of the Quad where the outdoor ceremony was to be held until his name was called, and then he could walk up on the stage and get his degree. Now, the night before, the department party was being hosted in his honor, but the honoree suddenly was noticeably absent.

The great poet seemed to have disappeared. He had edged toward the patio door, then was outside, where he lit a cigarette and looked around nervously. Members of the Wake Forest English Department had cause to celebrate: Professor Elizabeth Phillips was a favorite colleague, the first faculty member to have announced her arrival, in 1957, by sending out formal invitations for "cocktails." She subsequently became one of the first two women to become full professors at Wake Forest, and she wrote books on Poe, Dickinson, and Marianne Moore. Now she was hosting a homecoming for A.R. Ammons.

On that cool late spring evening the guests were greeted at the door by Elizabeth's housemate, Eva Rodtwitt, a Norwegian who had joined the Wake Forest faculty in 1966, liked to party, and was a professor of French. She kissed them on the lips, pinched their cheeks, and pushed them toward the food table. The poet somehow had escaped that familiar ritual popular with an otherwise taciturn department. In fact, he was slipping away, slowly, away from the patio and down the hill.

As if by design, Archie was met by our 4-year-old daughter, Sally, waiting for me in the woods between the two houses, who looked as shy as the poet, and was herself about to race away when he called out, "Hello." She stopped, turned around, and in the time it takes for a shy child to recognize a true friend, Archie was leaning over talking to her. He held out his hands to show her a flower he had picked along the way, and she studied it, smiled, and put it in her pocket. Then together they walked toward her house where, sitting on the steps of the back porch, they ignored the party laughter. Archie had come to stay, at least for a while.

This tender scene with our daughter Sally reminded me later of Archie's memory poem "Nelly Myers," an expression of his gratitude to a woman for whom his family had provided a room in their small farmhouse and who had loved him when he was a boy:

> she heard the tender blood in lips of children
>   and knew the hurt
>   and knew what to do:

The next morning as faculty lined up and students and parents took their places on the Quad, Archie stood in the shadows. President Gerald Ford, whose son Mike was graduating, gave the commencement address. Archie's family had joined President Ford and school dignitaries at the University luncheon. When the time came for the honorary degrees to be awarded and Archie's name was called, he came out of the shadows onto the stage, rather grim-faced, looked at his former teacher with barely a sign of recognition, shook Ed's hand, took the degree, and hurried off the stage. Within minutes he was in his car and on his way back to Ithaca. The reunion was complete.

photo by Susan Mullally, 1980, Critz, VA

: : :

At Cornell in 1973, when Archie received another letter from Ed, proposing that he consider a more extended visit to Wake Forest, he sat in his second floor office in Goldwin Smith Hall, staring out the window, and he must have wondered what trouble he had made for himself. He had mentioned Wake Forest to his friends who gathered at 9:00 a.m. in the coffee shop, called the Temple of Zeus, to hear him hold court. They were not especially impressed that he had received an honorary degree from a school they knew nothing about, but they hung on to whatever Archie had to say. Archie was a talker. They listened.

Archie's visit to Yale early in 1973 had been hosted by Harold Bloom, who secured for him an offer to join Yale's faculty. In February, he wrote Bloom that he was "disposed at the moment to accept the offer." He wrote but did not send a resignation letter to Cornell's English Department chair, Barry Adams, and another, also not sent, to accept the Yale offer. He formally rejected the Yale offer in March and soon thereafter began thinking seriously of a return to Wake Forest. In July, he wrote Josephine Miles, his poet friend he had met at Berkeley, "Why, I'm in pretty deep with a Southern university for the year 74-75 if all goes well." Perhaps it was easier to test out the idea on a Californian with less sense of the Mason-Dixon Line than a Cornellian. His most revealing expression about going home to North Carolina, however, came in a June 1973 letter to Bloom: "I have thought I would spend my sabbatic (year after next) in Winston-Salem where I might offer one seminar per semester at Wake Forest. That in order to see if I can live again in the South. The South is changed, and I might be able to do it. I have to get away from too close with magnificent universities."

Archie's return to Wake Forest for the honorary degree had surprised everyone, perhaps even himself; some of the faculty had never heard of him, 23 years after he had graduated at the original campus. It would be too much to say it was a complete success—considering Archie's stage fright and his disappearance from the reception in his honor—but he had liked the English Department, and they liked him. He had none of the posturing of some famous poets, and the faculty neither ignored nor flattered him—they just gravitated to one another in natural ways. Wake Forest was a very unpretentious, democratic place, where life was not much different from life on the old campus and it was plainspoken in its moral purpose—for much of its early history (since 1834) it had been a school for men training for the Baptist ministry. Archie,

COURTSEY OF JOHN R. AMMONS

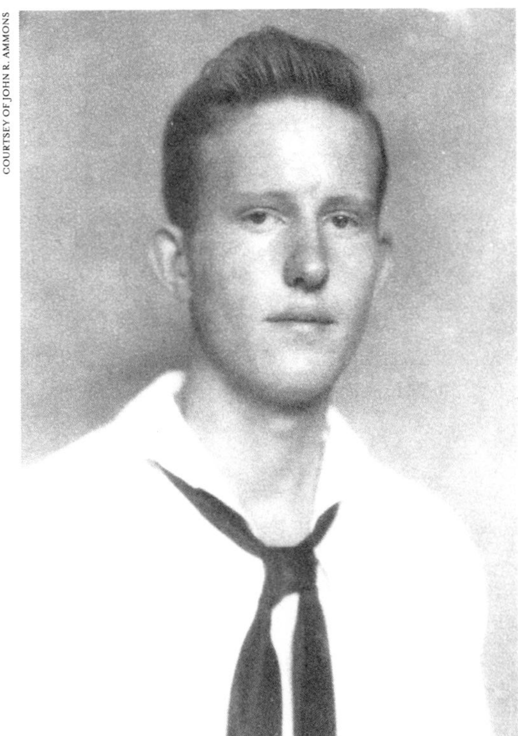

U.S. Navy 1945

not a ministerial student like so many others, had lived in a boarding house. He was the first in his family to go to college, and he had left a failed farm after coming out of the Navy in World War II to attend college on the G.I. Bill. He felt poor, but he had pride—his father was a landowner, not a tenant. In those post-war years, most small farms were failing. Archie hated farm work. He would try college.

Early in his first year at Wake Forest he dated his Spanish teacher, Phyllis Plumbo, who later became his wife and would make a home for him wherever they lived—Berkeley, California; Ocean City, New Jersey, where her family lived; and Ithaca, New York. Now, she was considering a short-term move to Winston-Salem (Archie always made the big decisions for the family), though she had only lived for a short time in the South, and she was afraid that she could not find all the ingredients she needed in the local grocery stores or find fresh vegetables she depended on at the Ithaca farmers market, the gastronomy for life in Ithaca.

COURTSEY OF JOHN R. AMMONS

Archie and John Ammons,
December 1973

: : :

And so Archie sat and stared out his window at the great Cornell campus of massive buildings, gardens, and rolling hills, where Nobel prize winners, waterfalls, and gorges vied for attention with views of Lake Cayuga. But there was something about Wake Forest that had both surprised and challenged him with its opportunities—he had always promised himself he would return to North Carolina—how easy it might be to renew his love of the land, and more than that, his love of family, the living and the dead. Now there was a special reason: he had a Cornell sabbatical coming up soon after he had renewed his relationship with his Wake Forest English teacher, now the University Provost, and he had met Ed's young family (our son was now six, the same age as Archie and Phyllis's John). Moreover, he had been impressed with how comfortably we lived, just a block from the lovely campus, and the smallness of the college had taken away some of the anxiety of travel, a lifelong travail. At Cornell Archie drove from home to his classes several miles, three or four times a day. Wake Forest was a residential walking campus with spacious lawns, bucolic fields, easy access to the quiet residential faculty neighborhood, the bank, the barber, the library, classrooms, the sundry shop, playing fields for his son, faculty lounges that were bee hives of talk—and no parking problems. He had been glad to see the new campus, and it had awakened feelings of gratitude he didn't know he had for his undergraduate years. Surrounded by the grandeur that is Cornell, he realized that Wake Forest in fact had had some good teachers and had given him his start. He thought of how many poems he had written out of memories of North Carolina, and he was flooded with images of those early years. No matter where he lived—New Jersey, California, New York—he remained close to his family and his memories of them and their land.

On Campus

"bring the man / home, to / acceptance of his place and time"

—*from* ***Tape for the Turn of the Year*** *by* A.R. AMMONS

A college campus, I believe, is the place where Archie and I found security because it is a place where we felt we could make our own way. We did not feel socially inferior. We were ambitious and competitive, willing to be judged on our own merits. As an undergraduate I was a student leader, which launched me as a lifetime community organizer. Archie was solitary, who needed time and place to write and to talk about ideas. On a college campus we both had the nerve to set our sights on marrying someone unlike anyone we had ever known—as a college freshman, he had the audacity to date his Spanish teacher, Professor Phyllis Plumbo, an exotic beauty, the daughter of an international businessman. As a graduate student, I set my sights on Dean Ed Wilson, 16 years my senior and a bachelor. Archie and I did not lack for confidence in matters of the heart. I did not hesitate to befriend a famous poet (Archie), and he did not hesitate to join "Emily's bandwagon," somewhat more social than he sometimes may have wished. We were free to be ourselves, where status was earned not inherited.

Archie and I both made friends easily and liked to talk; we could work our way around a college campus as if it had been made just for us. We were safe, mostly loved (I blush to put myself in his company), and together we were a force of nature—at least, I heard that we were. Archie put poetry on the map, especially at Wake Forest, where I moved traffic.

Each of us had felt class differences in our home towns—I living in my great-grandfather's old family house in a declining downtown neighborhood in Columbus, Georgia. Where we lived mattered a great deal in our teenage years, and our mother rented a small house in a suburban neighborhood so we could attend the high school for college-bound students; my daddy's used cars off his lot sat in our driveway, but oh, what a handsome man! Archie lived in a converted service station after his family left their broken fields for the nearby town of Chadbourn. At Whiteville High School especially Archie felt differences keenly between himself and the city children of big landowners and professionals. The one time he returned for a class reunion, he ignored the handshakes welcoming him home and congratulating him on his successes. His sisters seem not to have been so scarred.

Mona married and moved away and when interviewed about Archie said that they were not as poor as he said they were. Archie's point of pride was that they never took government checks—why, he wouldn't accept as much as a biscuit, a family member said. "We would have died before accepting welfare from anyone," Archie told one interviewer. Vida graduated from nursing school and was the office nurse in the private practice of a distinguished Whiteville doctor. She married a local landowner, Allen Cox, who had large farms, and they sent their three sons to state college. She has been one of the most prominent members of the Presbyterian Church and one of the best known people in Clarkton, close to Whiteville and now another diminished small town. She remains loyal to her place to this day. One son is one of the most successful farmers in the region. She was proud of her brother and anxious for local people to know his awards.

As for me, I made my way at Columbus High School into the ranks of the elected Junior Sub Debs, but it was by force of personality, not entitlement, and I didn't like it. I wanted out, and my friend Tita, daughter of a leading Columbus family, did, too. We both rebelled as cautiously as we dared and ended up in North Carolina, where we started over, she as a potter in Penland, I as a teacher and writer. When I came back once for a high school reunion, I blushed when a football player I had secretly admired introduced me to his wife as the friend who had helped him through Miss Cochran's English. I was a helper, not a leader, and helping was a role I enjoyed, but it didn't give me the freedom, the independence, I wanted. I found that in college, on campus.

Our families had some similarities. Both Archie and my daddy were boastful, Daddy still counting the football championships he had brought home to the Chattahoochee Valley and Archie still counting his money. Daddy had a lot of confidence because he acquired it when he was young and a star athlete in a category all of his own.

When Archie went to Cornell, after many years of adjusting, he became perhaps the most beloved professor on campus. Here his poetry mattered, and he was also accessible to everyone who walked through his open office door. He didn't take many risks as a faculty member—you couldn't always count on him to defend you, though he could surprise colleagues with a sudden spirited argument in faculty meetings. His risks were in poetry, willing to try anything, to act the fool or the philosopher, and to call out by names the poets he liked to parody. But socially, he was still guarded: at parties he joked and left as soon as he could. Country clubs made him (and me) nervous. Phyllis's background had prepared her to find her place easily among wives of the most prominent Cornell faculty members; she knew exactly how to host an elegant party, her tables laden with gourmet delights. They first lived in Ithaca in a charming small Cape Cod house on Hanshaw Road, a good address, then moved not far away to an even better address, among larger houses on Cayuga Heights Road, with gorgeous views of Cayuga Lake. Archie let her make the decisions. Phyllis had grown up accustomed to living in beautiful houses—after they returned from Berkeley and before they went to Cornell, they lived on the top floor of an impressive Plumbo home near the boardwalk at Atlantic City, New Jersey. He bought her a grand piano, which he liked to play. He had elegant taste in picking out art for her, and he appreciated the treasures she brought home from estate sales. But he didn't go in for fancy—he seemed always dressed in the same old corduroy jacks and slacks and typed on the same upright Underwood typewriter.

I think poetry brought out the best humanity in Archie, and although he rejected overt political poetry, his poem "Still" seems perfectly to reflect the best of American / Whitmanesque democracy (in sampling Whitman's most famous poem, he goes a step farther, to look beneath the leaves of grass) and I consider it the poem where we both meet. When I miss him most, I read it and of late, in this troubled world of inequalities, I read it often.

SPECIAL COLLECTIONS & ARCHIVES, Z. SMITH REYNOLDS LIBRARY, WAKE FOREST UNIVERSITY

Archie's Wake Forest graduation portrait, from *The Howler*

COURTSEY OF EMILY HERRING WILSON

Randall Jarrell teaching at UNC-G, Emily Herring Wilson, 3rd from right

Still

a poem by **A.R. AMMONS**

WHEN I GO BACK
TO MY
HOME COUNTRY

I said I will find what is lowly
      and put the roots of my identity
      down there:
each day I'll wake up
and find the lowly nearby,
         a handy focus and reminder,
a ready measure of my significance,
the voice by which I would be heard,
the wills, the kinds of selfishness
         I could
freely adopt as my own:

but though I have looked everywhere,
          I can find nothing
          to give myself to:
          everything is

magnificent with existence, is in
surfeit of glory:
nothing is diminished,
nothing has been diminished for me:

I said what is more lowly than the grass:
         ah, underneath,
         a ground-crust of dry-burnt moss:
         I looked at it closely
and said this can be my habitat: but
nestling in I
found
         below the brown exterior
         green mechanisms beyond the intellect
awaiting resurrection in rain: so I got up

and ran saying there is nothing lowly in the universe:
I found a beggar:
he had stumps for legs: nobody was paying
him any attention: everybody went on by:
        I nestled in and found his life:
there, love shook his body like a devastation:
I said
          though I have looked everywhere
          I can find nothing lowly
          in the universe:

I whirled through transfigurations up and down,
transfigurations of size and shape and place:
          at one sudden point came still,
          stood in wonder:
moss, beggar, weed, tick, pine, self, magnificent
          with being!

Hatteras, 1949–50

After graduating from Wake Forest College with a B.S. degree in 1949, Archie took his first teaching job in a small elementary school in Hatteras, on the easternmost tip of the state. It was isolated, and everybody knew everybody. He hadn't been in town an hour before news of the new teacher circulated. That fall, he and Phyllis, back home in New Jersey, exchanged frequent love letters. In November 1949, she wrote to him: "There is one thing that saddens me about our coming marriage—I will no longer receive your beautiful, touching letters. But I hope you will still write poetry to me, and if it is as inspired as the one I received yesterday, I will never want to share it with a single soul but you." She closes that letter: "Don't know which I prefer, writing to you, or dreaming about you. Time to dream now, as it's getting late." Over the Thanksgiving holiday, Archie and Phyllis were married in New Jersey, and she joined him in a small apartment over the Hatteras grocery store. She sang in the choir on Sundays; he played the piano and taught piano lessons. Walks on the shore in early morning and views in the evening fulfilled his desire for what he had called "the beautiful life" in his earliest courtship letters to Phyllis.

During one of their return visits to North Carolina, I arranged to drive Archie and Phyllis to Hatteras, where they were to meet some of his former students. He carried a snapshot of his eighth grade students in his wallet, and I thought it would be an adventure for them to see again the red-headed teacher who taught them to dance. But at the last minute, Archie backed out. My friend Jane Kelly, whose house Archie and Phyllis had stayed in during a visit to Winston-Salem, and I drove down the long, narrow NC Highway 12 to the remote village of Hatteras, and I was glad that he had not come with us. But I came away with a keen sense of the life he must have lived there, and I wrote a poem, published in Cornell's 2017 *Epoch* magazine.

C COLLECTION, PHOTOGRAPHIC ARCHIVES, UNC-CH

Downtown Hatteras, late 1940s

Archie's students at Hatteras Elementary School, 1950

OURTSEY OF JOHN R. AMMONS

"Hairpin"

a poem by **EMILY HERRING WILSON**

You watched your wedding gift to Phyllis—a refrigerator—
unloaded from the freight boat.
The morning was cold and windy. All week you said, "The
ocean's loud tonight."
She shivered and wished to go home to South Jersey, but the
die was cast:

You were the new school teacher, who rented rooms above
the grocery store.
On the narrow strip of land, you stood in the sound and spat
in the ocean.
Phyllis lacked for spices, good pots and pans, and a set of
kitchen knives,

Nothing she wanted in the Sears catalogue. The mail boat
brought her mother's lament:
Her oldest daughter had gone to the end of the world:
Hatteras, North Carolina,
Wherever that was, sliding into the deep,

The main road closed by mounds of sand, cut off, isolated,
marooned.
You played the piano, organized dances for your students,
and walked the beach.
When Phyllis took the prize for the Cake Walk, she was
embarrassed.

She had a fine singing voice, but her dark eyes were ringed
with suffering.
You wondered if she would stay, and she didn't, or not for
long. She would go home and wait.
The flag was raised at the weather station, a hurricane stirred
offshore.

The wooden land bridge rattled. After school, the children raced to the beach
even in winter. They ran up the narrow steps of the lighthouse like lizards.
Why, I've climbed it many a time, they bragged: you were fainthearted.

Yards were marked by tombstones, half-buried in the sand.
Mr. Austin's theatre was between his house and the Methodist parsonage.
His daughter Mona sold tickets to *Gone with the Wind*, her cousin ran the projector.

A stormy evening on a lonely island, a plantation and a fiery woman,
Scarlett, not a fisherman's wife who could choose a fish from any boat without paying for it.
Sunday morning calmed the waters, and you and your bride slept late.

Across Oregon Inlet the ferry rose and fell. You watched her departure from your window.
When Phyllis arrived home, she called on the only phone, everyone listening in the storeroom.
You could not tell her you had found a hairpin in the bed.

Mill Road School, class of 1938, Northfield, NJ. Phyllis Plumbo, 1st row, 4th from left.

NORTHFIELD NJ HISTORY MUSEUM

COURTESY OF JOHN R. AMMONS

Phyllis Plumbo teaching Spanish at Wake Forest College, 1947

Archie and Phyllis at the reception for Phyllis's sister Mary's wedding in New Jersey, 1951

COURTSEY OF JOHN R. AMMONS

Archie,
about 14 years old,
Columbus County,
a photo
his sister Vida
treasured

COURTESY OF JOHN R. AMMONS

Archie,
in the early 1950s

COURTESY OF JOHN R. AMMONS

"Ten Years Ago I Was,"

by A.R. AMMONS, BERKELEY, CALIFORNIA, MAY 1951

Ten years ago I was an ignorant boy on a poor farm in one of the most undeveloped areas of the United States. No electricity, none of the "modern conveniences" (also, however, none of the modern hysterias). It seems, as I look back, that the earlier part of my life must have taken place in a remote century, the sixteenth or seventeenth. All this in so few years.

The age of white washed fireplaces, where we used to get white clay from beside the road, where the road machine had dug out the ditches, to perform this duty with, every other Saturday.

I believe I would not be wasting my time in trying to recollect some of those days and write down some incidents from them. For instance, the tobacco-barn tender is no more, and (thank God) now that oil burners are available.

Incidents: The life story of Silver.
Drowning biddies (chicks) during night showers
The history of the tobacco barn.
The old wooden school; including the various attempts on the part of the boys to burn it down.
The Spring Meadow.
The killing of the 'coon one Sunday afternoon at Jim Sumerset's.
The history of the Blake Owl.
The Syrup-biscuit.
The Episode of the Rupture-Cure.
Malaria.
The Wildcat Episode; or Swimming in February.
Stories of my father.
The Secret; or my first pride: Doshie Holcomb and the borrowing of the thread.
The Money Huts; or My Father's Mysterious Powers.

I could go on endlessly, but it's one o'clock a.m. But these little titles represent to me a much richer life than that I live today, however unbearable it might have been in many respects.

A Sabbatical Question, 1973

"Call me down from the / high places"
*—from "**Pray Without Ceasing**" by* A.R. AMMONS

In 1964, Archie began his teaching career at Cornell, on a temporary appointment. His road to Ithaca had been unexpected and unlikely—from the North Carolina farm to the college campus to Berkeley, California, where after marriage and at Phyllis's urging they went after Hatteras. He enrolled in undergraduate classes at UC-Berkeley to make up for deficiencies in English and began work toward a master's degree. She had spent summers in Berkeley working on a Master's in Spanish and had loved it. But he was anxious. Although he was writing poems he shared with friends and the poet Josephine Miles, whom he met soon after enrolling in classes, the sophisticated culture of classmates and classes unnerved him. His father was not well, and he felt drawn toward home. After two years, interrupted in the summers, he made the decision to leave, and although Phyllis urged him to go back to North Carolina, he took a job in her family's glass business in New Jersey. He explained it this way to her: "I needed your father." And so they moved into the upstairs apartment of the Plumbos' capacious house on the boardwalk at Atlantic City. "Miserable," he said, as "a fish out of water," he did well enough in business, but after he gave a poetry reading at Cornell in 1963, he was invited back as a lecturer, and he leapt at the chance. As he published one book of poems after another—*Corsons Inlet* and *Tape for the Turn of the Year* in 1965; *Northfield Poems* in 1966; *Uplands* in 1970; *Briefings* in 1971; and *The Collected Poems* in 1972—he became one of the best known faculty members on the campus. Why should he consider leaving, even for a short time?

The more he thought about Ed's offer for his sabbatical, the more daunting the move seemed to be. It was wrong to take his young son, John, away from his friends; he had other offers to consider (notably, Yale's and Harold Bloom's); he had obligations to Cornell, where, despite being the only member of the department without an advanced degree, he had within a few years been made a full professor. He was proud of the reception Cornell had given him.

And yet he was taken with the offer to act on his impulse to go home to North Carolina, and to keep at the same time his ties to Cornell. A compromise of sorts was worked out: Archie would spend his upcoming

SPECIAL COLLECTIONS & ARCHIVES, Z. SMITH REYNOLDS LIBRARY, WAKE FOREST UNIVERSITY

Ed Wilson at Wake Forest University

sabbatical, for the 1974–75 academic year, at Wake Forest. He and Ed agreed that he would teach one writing course a semester while living with Phyllis and John in the faculty neighborhood, our neighborhood.

What I now view as truly remarkable is that Archie did accept this appointment as Visiting Professor of English. His 1967 sabbatical to Rome on a Guggenheim (with their newly adopted infant son: what were they thinking?) had ended abruptly after several months when he couldn't stand another day—he hated the pretense of Old Europe, it took too long to get mail, and they couldn't find the right baby bottle for John. The one time he had flown, in the early 1950s, home from California to see his father, he had been so terrified that he swore that he would never fly again. So for the Guggenheim, the family traveled by ship to Europe and returned to the States by ship, apparently a rough passage home, which terrified Archie and Phyllis—although John loved it.

Despite travel always being a bold and daunting move, Archie decided to give it a go—back to North Carolina. I think what most drew him was that he wanted to be near his sisters and the family graveyard. I think he also respected his teacher, Ed Wilson, and appreciated that Ed had reached out to him with a job offer and a willingness to meet his requirements as no one else in North Carolina had done. And I think he began to trust me to work out the bumps in the road.

Sabbatical, 1974–75, part 1

"The perfect journey is no need to go"
*—from **The Snow Poems** by* A.R. AMMONS

And so Archie agreed to spend his 1974–75 Cornell sabbatical teaching a writing course each semester in the English Department of Wake Forest, rented Don and Meyressa Schoonmaker's house at 2090 Royall Drive, and off they went, leaving Ithaca on an early August morning in his 1972 red Chevrolet, headed south. About ten hours later, Phyllis unpacked her kitchen utensils, John arranged his collections in his bedroom next to his parents', and Archie looked out the broad living room windows on the back of the house and took some interest in the trees and hedges and a creek.

Should he worry about flooding? He was assured that they were safe. (In later years, in fact, the creek flooded.)

But a week had not passed before Archie had second and third thoughts about the move. He began to complain to me that a noise at night was keeping him awake, and he would have to leave.

I said, Not so fast. What kind of noise?

Mechanical.

Where?

Over there, pointing to the east where the tobacco factories ran night shifts.

I'll need to hear it, I said.

He scowled.

About midnight? I asked.

He nodded and slammed the door.

That night after everyone was sleeping in my house, I drove two blocks to Archie's and it was quiet as a mouse, though I wouldn't have said "mouse"—it would have given him ideas about noises in the night. I turned off the engine and waited: nothing except the Becks' barking dog, who went back to sleep. There were no lights on in Archie's house; perhaps he was sleeping, too. But I was taking no chances. I took the brake off and rolled down the hill, until I turned on the ignition and eased on down the road. Even the fraternity houses were quiet. Just as I started to give it up, I thought I heard a humming, not loud but steady. I turned onto Reynolds Park Boulevard and made my way toward the nearby factories. I rolled down the window, and the hum was definitely louder. Within a mile, I had come to what might be the disturbance, but the factory was dark. I pulled to the side of the road and listened again.

Ah, there was a persistent humming, which after an hour was also keeping me awake. I made a note of the time and place and drove home.

The next morning I called a friend of mine, a Wake Forest trustee, who was an officer at R.J. Reynolds Tobacco. He answered his own phone, which seemed promising (in those faraway days). I explained that we had a famous poet living on campus being kept awake at night by a noise I had traced to a Reynolds factory on the boulevard. He may have laughed, but it was not a mean laugh.

I suppose poets are sensitive, he reflected. Let me see what I can find out.

The next day he called to say that a cooling fan perhaps was the culprit, and he had asked that it be turned off at night. I shuddered: how many workers would breathe stale air to satisfy one sensitive poet?

But my friend assured me that the building was empty at night, no problem, just let him know how things went.

Several days later I went by to see Archie after class, stopping in the kitchen to confer with Phyllis. He hadn't heard the noise, he had slept well. But John had sneezed, more than once. There would be a whole new set of allergens here in the South. Not to worry, I assured Archie; John was unaware he had sneezed.

The next week I had a local doctor, another friend, drop by to welcome the Ammonses to Winston-Salem. He took casual note of John, running in and out of the house with neighborhood boys—Eddie, Burton, Stuart, Davie, and Stevie. As he left, he congratulated Phyllis and Archie on having such a handsome son and said to give him a call should they need him, but he was certain John was one of the healthiest children he had ever seen.

: : :

Archie had chosen a good location. Not only were there lots of boys John's age in the neighborhood (all invited to his 9th birthday party in January and a performance by Jim Dodding, a member of the theatre department, who did magic tricks) and faculty wives for Phyllis to do what Archie described as "running around," but Tom and Louise Gossett and their cat, Napper Tandy, lived directly across the street. Archie went over every day to read aloud some of his poems. Tom was an English professor at Wake Forest, Louise at Salem College, the historic women's college in scenic Old Salem (one of the first places new friends took Phyllis). Louise especially was a keen reader of poetry. Tom, in his gentle voice, rose to the occasion admirably to offer his own interpretations. And Napper Tandy meowed approval in the background. (Tapes of these informal readings have become part of Special Collections in the Z. Smith Reynolds Library at Wake Forest.)

In his campus office, Archie had been surprised to discover that it was unlike Cornell, where most faculty members did not hang out in the lounge. English colleagues at Wake Forest congregated for coffee and conversation in their lounge (which in 2001 would be named the A.R. Ammons Lounge), and their numbers increased. In no time, laughter rang out up and down the hall. Archie Ammons was a very funny fellow—bawdy, too. Even faculty members who hadn't been seen outside their offices in weeks wandered by, stopped, looked in, and took a turn at refilling the coffee maker.

Class, friends, poetry, Napper Tandy, and Phyllis's hot coffee and pastries, for which I was invited almost every afternoon, provided an essential routine that Archie soon fell into with something like ease. I waited like an expectant child for Archie to walk home from the office. We smoked cigarettes and argued about the failures of the South, changing sides whenever one of us got the better of the other, and talking about our native states when they needed defending. Sometimes he listened to a local talk radio show and paced back and forth, threatening to call and give listeners his two-cents worth about the government, but losing nerve at the last minute. I was relieved: I was a liberal Democrat who never saw a government program to help the least advantaged that I didn't like. He was a political agnostic—he didn't like government help in any form and never voted. We argued at some length, and when with such intensity, I cried, he would be startled and back off. Archie had a gentle side, soft as Napper Tandy's purr.

ARCHIE R. AMMONS PAPERS DIVISION OF RARE AND MANUSCRIPT COLLECTIONS, CORNELL UNIVERSITY LIBRARY

L to R: Emily Herring Wilson, Archie, Josephine Jacobsen, Harold Bloom, at the Bollingen Prize celebration, December 1974, at Wake Forest University, published in the Wake Forest University student newspaper *The Old Gold and Black.*

COURTSEY OF JOHN R. AMMONS

For Emily Wilson, from a Newcomer

a poem by A.R. AMMONS

When it gets hot here it's really noticeable:
clumps of copperheads unwind,
brotherly younglings, and form separate

rings of attention: maypop blossoms
stretch wide open, nearly closing back on
themselves: black widows, keyed up,

traipse their mates off to dinner:
squirrels sail onto branches tailbone
fine and, swaying, hull nuts: joe-pye

two-men tall on the creek banks blooms,
bonnets as pink and wide as parasols: but
Emily spells welcome warmer than any weather.

Emily at the zenith of her life as a political activist, at Hyde Park, 2017, with sculpture of Eleanor Roosevelt

photo by
Susan Mullally,
Reynolda House,
1981

A Day Trip Interrupted

As Archie became more comfortable in his new surroundings, I took more liberties in presuming to include our families in more activities: supper together in our homes, after which Archie read poems aloud; a picnic at Jane and Pat Kelly's nearby cabin on the Yadkin River; Phyllis's cooking class for friends at my house to teach us to make French bread; and walks in Reynolda Gardens. Perhaps I was taking too many liberties when one of my invitations backfired. This was the day:

We had been driving for more than an hour, on our way up to the small North Carolina town of Sparta, where we were to go to the house of Peggy and Wally Carroll, whose Winston-Salem *Journal-Sentinel* had won the 1971 Pulitzer for environmental reporting. I had promised Archie a mountain view, Phyllis had packed a picnic, and their John and our Eddie were happily laughing in the back seat of Archie's car. I was leading in my car with Ed and our daughters, Sally and Julie.

Wally and Peggy had invited other guests who knew of Archie's fame in poetry and Phyllis's bread. They had built a wonderful house on the top of a mountain, and the cool air and spectacular landscape promised North Carolina at her best. I kept Archie in my rearview mirror, and I sped up when he seemed about to climb into my trunk. Ed dozed, the children talked. I imagined our idyllic picnic, when a horn started blasting, and I jumped. I saw in the mirror that Archie was waving his arm out the window and had pulled off the road and was turning around.

I turned around, got out of my car and went to his window. He was red in the face and cursing: "You promised me no more than an hour up this God-forsaken country." He glared. "I am not driving another mile!"

"Are you kidding me?" I asked. "We are expected. You accepted."

He glared.

Phyllis looked apologetic and handed over the picnic basket to me.

"I will never trust you again," he snapped.

I stepped back from his car, and he sped away.

Sabbatical, part 2

The next occasion that went bust was not my doing. Archie and Phyllis had been invited for dinner at a private club, and they had accepted. Ed and I, knowing his hosts, were included in the invitation. It began on a very awkward note.

The host taunted Archie with probing questions about why he had left North Carolina, insisting that he had sold out to the North. It is a taunt Southerners sometimes lob at those who have left, and I hoped that Archie would demolish him. To my surprise, Archie said nothing, his ears seemed to flatten, and his face turned pink. He kept silent. I held my breath, the evening passed, and we did not speak directly of it afterwards.

I was surprised that given such a ready-made opportunity to defend himself, Archie had passed on it, but I was glad that we had not made a scene, because I was embarrassed. I think he was embarrassed, too. He didn't like stress—he had enough of his own. Although we both were well known for speaking our minds, we also picked our battles. We did not want to take a foolish risk when nothing would come of it. At the members-only club we had placed ourselves in an untenable position—sitting down as guests at the table of a pompous man, giving him a certain power to insult us and not wanting to be rude ourselves. Archie and I held on tight when we felt threatened. That night I was policing the joint as his protector, but I failed to see it coming. Although we kept our composure, we both were hurt, and we drove home in silence. Phyllis, whose hearing had become increasingly less sharp, apparently had heard none of it. Just as well.

After a few weeks of social successes and failures, Archie took matters into his own hands and devised means of taking care of himself: suppers at the K&W Cafeteria, a family-owned business since 1937. The K&W was Archie's favorite place to eat, as it was ours, and Phyllis and John and we went with him. Winston-Salem is close to small towns and rural neighborhoods, and many working families love the K&W. The food is great—steam tables of meats, vegetables, salads, breads, desserts, and beverages, served by older women in hair nets calling out, "H'ep you?" as the line moves past. It is Southern cooking at its best.

COURTSEY OF JOHN R. AMMONS

Eddie Wilson (L) and John Ammons at the Wilsons' house, 1975

But what pleased Archie most was a little game he and Phyllis devised. At the K&W you could pay for the first cup of coffee and take the empty cup back and get a free refill. Archie and Phyllis figured out how to take advantage of the offer pretty quickly—one of them would buy a cup of coffee (and it was hot enough to suit them), drink it with the meal, and then pass the cup to the other, who would take it for a free refill. I think it wasn't just saving money that they liked, although they did like the modest prices of the K&W. It was a sort of game, and for Archie, making and saving money was a serious game. I often wondered if any good country people had figured out how to play it at the K&W, and I sometimes was caught watching customers refill their cups. As far as I ever saw, however, it was a balding red-headed fellow who could have been a farmer who most often took his empty cup to the refill station.

On the early evenings when the Wilsons and the Ammonses had supper at the K&W, Archie left in an unusually relaxed mood.

Interlude: Two Poems

Meanwhile, Archie was writing poems. He had brought along his old Underwood typewriter and set up shop at home and began to write. He wrote "For Emily Wilson" one Saturday morning when the house was quiet. He had declined our invitation to accompany me and Phyllis to the nearby farmers market, and when we came home, after an hour or so, he presented me with a newly minted poem. The next week, he had one for Ed.

SPECIAL COLLECTIONS & ARCHIVES, Z. SMITH REYNOLDS LIBRARY, WAKE FOREST UNIVERSITY

The Asheville writers club sponsored John LeCarre's reading at Salem College and asked Ed to introduce him.
photo by Susan Mullally

For Edwin Wilson

a poem by **A.R. AMMONS**

Did wind and wave design the albatross's wing,
honed compliances: or is it effrontery to
suggest that the wing designed the gales and

seas: are we guests here, then, with all the
gratitude and soft-walking of the guest:
provisions and endurances of riverbeds,

mountain shoulders, windings through of tulip
poplar, grass, and sweet-frosted foxgrape:
are we to come into these and leave them as

they are: are the rivers in us, and the slopes,
ours that the world's imitate, or are we
mirrorments merely of a high designing aloof

and generous as a host to us: what would
become of us if we declined and staked out
a level affirmation of our own: we wind

the brook into our settlement and husband the
wind to our sails and blades: what is to
be grateful when let alone to itself, as for

a holiday in naturalness: the albatross, ah,
fishes the waves with a will beyond the
waves' will, and we, to our own doings, put

down the rising of sea or mountain slope: except
we do not finally put it down: still, till
the host appears, we'll make the masters here.

For Emily Wilson

a poem by A.R. AMMONS

WHEN I GO BACK
TO MY
HOME COUNTRY

Such a long time as the wave idling gathers
lofts and presses forward into the curvature
of the height before one realizes that the

tension completes itself with a fall through air,
disorganization the prelude to the meandering
of another gather and hurl, the necessary:

ah, what can one make to absorb the astonishment:
you should have seen me the merchant at market
this morning: the people ogled me with severe

goggles: maids, buying in manners and measures
beyond themselves, stared into my goods and
then grew horror-eyed: wives still as distant

from day as a carrot from dinner took the
misconnection sagely, a usual patience:
peashells, I said, long silky peashells: cobs,

I said, long cobs: husks and shucks, I said:
one concerned person pointed out that my whole
economy was wrong; yes, I said, but I have

nothing else to sell: and I said to her, won't
you appreciate the silky beds where seeds
have lain: she had not come to that: and

how about this residence all the grains have
left: won't you buy it and think about it:
not for dinner, she said: rinds, I cried,

rinds and peelings: there was some interest
in those, as for a marmalade, but no one willing,
finally, to do the preparations: absurd, one

woman shouted, and then I grew serious: can you
do with that: but she was off before we fully
met: you should have seen me the merchant at

market this morning: will bankruptcy make a
go of it: will the leavings be left only: the
wave turns over and does not rise again, that wave.

Sabbatical, part 3

Archie was very generous with his time—he not only saw his students after class, some of them following him home for Phyllis's pastries, but he read after supper in people's homes, and he read poems that strangers dropped in his office box. In fact, he was so generous that we began to stretch the terms of his contract and asked that he allow us to make him the center of a public celebration for his having just been awarded the Bollingen Prize in Poetry for *Sphere: The Form of a Motion*. It was so unusual for us to have such a notable prize-winner in literature that we wanted to boast a bit, and besides, by then many of us loved him like an old friend. I put myself in charge of the event (I have made a career out of organizing literary events for public audiences). Archie told me that it didn't mean much to him—that when he had needed recognition, he didn't get any, and now it didn't matter. I'd add "as much." It mattered to be chosen in a list of previous winners that included W. H. Auden, Ezra Pound, Wallace Stevens, Robert Frost, and John Ashbery, the contemporary poet Archie admired the most. He agreed that we could put on an event if we insisted, and he suggested that Harold Bloom and Josephine Jacobsen might be invited to speak. Both accepted our invitation.

Harold Bloom was one of the best known literary critics in America and to have him at Wake Forest was exciting. Archie had agreed that if Harold would come, he'd be glad to see him. The poet Josephine Jacobsen, who lived in Baltimore, had been one of the first poets to reach out to Archie in the early 1960s when he was just beginning to publish. Bloom had been writing discursive pieces about Archie and had almost single-handedly named him master of the house of American poetry, though soon Helen Vendler of Harvard was to match Bloom in the importance she gave to Ammons's work. And so it was arranged that Harold Bloom and Josephine Jacobsen would be on our campus in early December 1974, the program to be held in DeTamble Auditorium, small enough, I thought, not to alarm him.

On the day of the Wake Forest seminar honoring Archie, I and a gathering of English professors escorted him and the two distinguished lecturers for lunch at a nearby eatery called the Village Tavern. In deference to its name, it was dark and cozy, and a wood fire settled in the grate, knocking off the season's chill. After a scramble among the men to assist Jacobsen in removing her cashmere wrap, she resisted all efforts and tightened it about her shoulders and sat down. She had arrived on the afternoon plane from Baltimore and expressed a wish to go to her room to prepare for the evening. Archie protested that there would be no good time without her, and to please tell him about her husband, Eric, and their family's tea business.

She smiled and said all was well.

Someone turned over his water glass, the waitress mopped up, and things were off to a difficult start. Anyone overhearing what faculty members talked about would have been disappointed. It was, as best I could make out, a conversation about teeth—cavities and crowns—Archie's subject of first resort, and often his favorite topic at Cornell's coffee shop, informally known as the Temple of Zeus, located in the basement of Goldwin Smith Hall. Then the tempo of the Ammons-Bloom talk quickened past cavities and crowns to criticism and lofty praise for each other, laced with occasional gossip. Josephine was silent and looked shy as a plain little bird that had been blown into a zoo.

The orders were placed, fries and burgers were served, and Archie sent his coffee back to be heated.

Josephine whispered to me, "Could you take me home?"

I was startled. "When?" I asked.

"Now," she insisted, standing up.

"Of course," I said, and not a minute too soon.

Archie suddenly was very attentive, and he stood and said, "Are we finished?"

I said, "I'll come back for you guys and pay the check" and Archie laughed, and I hurried Josephine out the door.

In the car Josephine said, "I mean I want to go home to Baltimore. I'm no match for Professor Bloom," but she had a sly smile at the same time.

And I said, "Nonsense. You'll hit a home run."

And so she stayed, and so she did.

: : :

At the seminar Bloom took the stage and began at once reading a long, extremely demanding paper called "A.R. Ammons: The Breaking of Vessels." In it he argued that *Sphere* was Archie's "most remarkable achievement to date." It was vintage Bloom—intellectual, confident, and instructive—telling Archie what he should and should not do. We shifted in our seats. Perhaps he had misjudged the occasion. This was not a meeting of the MLA; it was a hometown parade for a local hero, with two of the best friends a poet could have—none smarter than Harold Bloom, none more sensitive than Josephine Jacobsen. But the two of them were of different minds: Bloom had come to judge Ammons; Jacobsen, to praise.

The audience was attentive to the great man, and within minutes, he was speaking in tongues, as mystifying as the Firebrand Pentecostal Holiness Church Archie had attended as a boy, and sweating profusely. Then he threw off his jacket. Then he undid his tie.

Startled, I whispered to Archie, quivering on the back row beside me, "He is going to be naked soon."

Archie did not answer.

Bloom-speak was hard for most of the audience to follow—what exactly was "the geometry of the Ammonsian heterocosm"?

Although Archie seemed to be too agitated to be listening, in fact, I think he may have been the only one who understood exactly what Bloom was saying—Bloom was "lecturing" him about ways he was going in the wrong direction in his poetry and about what turn-arounds he should execute. Finally, it seemed it would never end, but it did, with a soft landing in the last lines of Archie's poem called "The Arc Inside and Out," dedicated to Harold Bloom, the last poem in *Collected Poems 1951–71*: *Every morning the sun comes, the sun*. At last, something that we could understand. The audience applauded. Clint McCown, one of Archie's Wake Forest students, was sitting next to Archie and sensed his discomfort when Archie growled, "My God, he is going to ask me to come up on the stage." Bloom did, and Archie went, but it was the briefest of moments and then Archie was back down the aisle.

The evening was quite a contrast from the afternnon's presentation by the lovely, gracious Josephine Jacobsen, herself no slouch in the intellect department. A calm had settled over the audience as her soft voice gained in strength. She had chosen to talk about *Tape for the Turn of the Year*, which Archie had published in 1965 and dedicated to his earliest supporters, Josephine and Elliott Coleman. *Tape* was a book-length poem that had been written on an adding machine tape. But Josephine had discovered in it a love poem, and when she closed with an excerpt from it, there was a sigh of relief and satisfaction—and a standing ovation. Josephine blushed, Bloom smiled with the charm of a school boy.

: : :

After Archie's brief stage appearance that night, he motioned Phyllis to follow him, and they could not be found. However, he recovered in time for a reception at the president's house (James Ralph and Betty Scales, great fans of the Ammonses, were on leave and Ed and I were using the house for entertaining). It didn't start well. I had ordered the food from the university caterer, and when Phyllis, a gourmet cook, took one look at it, she removed her jacket, asked for an apron, told us to get out of her way, and started finding utensils and pans in the kitchen drawers. She went to work on the meal, we kept the wine flowing, the gathering began to talk in language that Marianne Moore called "what plain American dogs and cats can read," and in an hour Phyllis presented a beautifully reconstructed meal for a seated dinner.

A photo from that event shows me and Bloom looking at Archie, Archie looking at Josephine, and Josephine looking off in the distance. Everyone looks sweet and sly and slightly amused. Never has so much tension been resolved in such a show of innocence. At the reception, the public event was considered to be over. Archie was able to relax and be himself. I think that Robert Morgan, a North Carolina native and Cornell colleague of Archie's, said it best when he observed that the excellence of Ammons's poetry was the "high abstraction of his thought wedded to a living voice." Bloom in brilliant fashion discussed the "Ammonsian sublime." Josephine talked about Archie's feelings, and her reading of a passage from *Tape for the Turn of the Year* will never be forgotten by those in the audience that day. She hit a home run so high that Archie's words must still be hanging in the sky over a quiet college campus, where poetry has many readers—the lesson Archie had come to teach us.

This is one passage from *Tape for the Turn of the Year* that Josephine Jacobsen read that day:

Josephine Jacobsen,
Wake Forest University, 1974
photo by Susan Mullally

who are you, deeper?
have I sounded you? was
that
bottom I struck? but oh
up in the heart & around
your breasts
   and to speak of the deep
   in your eyes, have
   I come into your
           measure? are
you getting yours? have
you been had?
you've had me: I float
   every cell
   comes to this:
           you are
beautiful: you are
just beautiful:
beautiful, thank you.

The Nickelodeon

After the Bollingen evening, Archie Ammons was the talk of the department, and more visitors asked to sit in on his class. He became a popular teacher, readings in the lounges were well attended, and then one day a new wrinkle was added by the Pied Piper of Poetry: Archie began running off a one-page mimeographed sheet of poems with submissions from faculty and students called *The Nickelodeon* (it sold for five cents), and people waited at the door of the closet where Archie grinned while the mimeograph machine spit copies out. He enjoyed thinking of clever ways to mark the price—*5 cents a sht, 5 cents a piece, 5 centers per, 5 shents a sot, 5 pennies for 3 pushes, unplgyr Nickel*—the same play at work in his poems. Archie loved being teacher, editor, and publisher, and *The Nickelodeon* made literary history at Wake Forest. Not only were poets in his classes published in it, but faculty members who were reclusive were suddenly turning up for readings and—behold—submitting their poems. I think especially of the Shakespearean scholar Doyle Fosso and the popular teacher Lee Potter, whose verses Archie liked very much. In the annals of Wake Forest literary history, researchers should take a look at *The Nickelodeon*, which continued for some years after Archie got it started.

It wasn't the only playful idea Archie came up with that year. According to Clint McCown, Archie suggested that a group of poets write a poem every day and get together in the lounge to discuss it. Each poet was to put $2 in the pot, and they would discuss the poems, and then vote on the best and the winner would take away the prize money. Archie sometimes won, but not always. It was a rowdy and wonderful way to end the day.

There were other planned occasions. Near the Wake Forest campus is the Reynolda House Museum of American Art, the former home of the tobacco tycoon R.J. Reynolds and his wife, Katherine Smith Reynolds, and their children, where visitors came to see the collection of art and furnishings and to attend public events, including poetry readings. Archie was a frequent visitor at Reynolda House during his sabbatical year, invited by Nick Bragg, the executive director and a great admirer of Archie's. Maria Ingram, a Winston-Salem poet, and I had organized a new group called The Tenth Muse and we were building an audience for poetry. I wrote poems on a Smith Corona electric typewriter, my high school graduation present, after the children had gone to bed. My undergraduate studies with Randall Jarrell had unnerved me and I had lost my confidence as a poet. His commentaries in class about the poets he admired—Gerard Manley Hopkins, Marianne Moore, T.S. Eliot, Robert Frost—were intense, so different from Archie's relaxed classes. I felt a new desire to write and began to send out individual poems Archie had liked and got some of them accepted. Then I began to create a manuscript. Archie suggested that I think about starting my own small press, and Betty Leighton, Isabel Zuber, and I, who had been meeting once a week in our Secret Writers Club to write together, thought it was a great idea. It would give us something to do after Archie returned to Ithaca, and so Jackpine Press was born.

Betty Scales, the President's wife, gave us office space in the president's house, and we sent out an appeal for subscribers, an idea I borrowed from Virginia Woolf and Hogarth Press. We would get supporters to send us $100 each, and we would send them our books as they were published. Archie suggested that we begin with my own poems, for which I had built a small following, and we began with my *Balancing on Stones*, back when local reviews in North Carolina newspapers were good enough to sell a local book. Fred Chappell, on the MFA faculty at the University of North Carolina at Greensboro, was always especially generous to new poets. Archie recommended a long poem by one of his Cornell students, *Orion*, by Jerald Bullis, which we published. And then we chose *Sidetracks*, by Clint McCown, who had studied with Archie at Wake Forest, and who said that Jackpine launched him on his career in poetry and fiction; he would become head of the MFA program at Virginia Commonwealth University. We were the first to publish Jeff Daniel Marion, who would become a much recognized Tennessee poet. Our most successful publication, however, was the first book of fiction by a nationally known writer, Josephine Jacobsen, our Archie connection. Her stories, *A Walk with Raschid*, was well reviewed and got national attention. Best of all, she and I became lifelong friends. Ed and I and our children visited Josephine and her husband, Eric, at their mountain house in Whitefield, New Hampshire, and in their historic row house in Baltimore, where they took us to lunch at the Johns

Hopkins Faculty Club. Josephine returned on a number of visits to Winston-Salem (once to spend the night with me in Jane Kelly's cabin on the Yadkin River, where we talked poetry into the early hours of the dawn), and I went to see her in Maryland at the Kendal retirement community outside Baltimore.

Jackpine Press started with friends—Isabel, Betty, Archie, and me—and was supported by friends. Among our greatest supporters was Professor Germaine Bree, the distinguished French critic, who after a career at the University of Wisconsin came to Wake Forest as our first Kenan Professor. She and Archie were great admirers of one another. It was a magical time for literature at Wake Forest.

But the press wasn't to last. We paid our bills but we couldn't pay ourselves. Still, the Jackpine Press caused a little stir in small press circles and was a sort of darling of the lit set in Winston-Salem. We didn't have a plan, however, and when Archie left to go back to Cornell, he would lose interest in meeting all our expectations about finding new writers and providing blurbs for their books, and things began to fall apart. I began to write nonfiction, and in time Isabel and I withdrew officially from Jackpine, and Betty carried it on. She was especially successful in publishing Josephine Jacobsen's second book of stories, *Adios, Mr. Moxley*. Jackpine Press was a start-up before there were start-ups. We were not entrepreneurs. We were friends. And it was fun.

The hours we spent talking things through with Archie, printing our first brochures, accepting our first manuscripts, hosting our first book parties—they were wondrous. And the fact that we published my own book of poems, *Balancing on Stones*, was a boost to my confidence and my love of poetry. I had had a bad case of nerves after publishing a chapbook, *Down Zion's Alley*, a few years earlier, and thought that I would never again expose myself so publicly to readers. Archie helped me overcome my fears. When I stopped writing poetry to teach and to write nonfiction, Archie said, "You can be as good in poetry as you want to be, but there are other things that interest you more now." (The poet in our group he admired the most was Isabel Zuber.) That was true—I still wrote poems, but not as seriously. I began to write women's histories—*Hope and Dignity: Older Black Women of the South* was my first—which appealed to my activist nature. But he might also have said that writing poetry was something I had done with him, and I knew there would not be another time in my life when writing poetry was such a personal triumph for my spirit.

COURTSEY OF JOHN R. AMMONS

**Archie at home,
Cayuga Heights Road**

COURTSEY OF JOHN R. AMMONS

Phyllis and Archie
in front of their house
on Cayuga Heights Road

The Bread and Butter of Life

a poem by EMILY HERRING WILSON

Phyllis makes magic:
add, stir, knead, and
under a light cloth
life rises, waits.
She brings perfection
to the table, without
fanfare, lets it speak
for itself.
If God were hungry,
He'd have Phyllis for his wife!
She has the touch
no man
can do without.
Her bread's
the envy
of the neighborhood
and rises
in the dreams
of other women.

Day Trip to Old Wake Forest

On a lovely sunny day we took a trip to the original Wake Forest campus, near Raleigh in Wake County, where Archie and Ed had been student/teacher after they both returned from WWII. The return to the old campus seemed to put Archie in a relaxed, even sentimental mood. He enjoyed walking around the campus with Ed, while Vida and Phyllis and I sat on one of the benches and remarked on the beauty of the campus, encircled by a low stone wall. The old Alumni Building where Ed had taught Archie had been torn down, but the chapel and other academic buildings were in good repair, and Ed and Archie wandered through. We went downtown to the popular café called Shorty's, and it hadn't changed much in all those years. The boys were still racking up pool balls for a game in the back room, though the campus is now home to the Southeastern Baptist Theological Seminary, and life is much quieter. Archie and Ed talked about the old campus, and memories returned.

They sat by the Old Well, relaxed, companionable, remembering the way it was.

"Why did we ever leave?" Archie asked.

"Money, of course," Ed said.

The Wake Forest Medical School, founded in 1902, had been in Winston-Salem since 1939. Then the Z. Smith Reynolds Foundation offered a large tract of land for a new campus in Winston-Salem near Reynolda House and a promise to build buildings, as well as to provide a monetary gift in perpetuity, for the rest of the college to follow. For some, it was the chance of a lifetime to take a small college to national prominence, which Wake Forest has certainly achieved in Winston-Salem. For others, it was heartbreak, leaving a place so beloved. But Ed, returning from graduate school, joined the faculty making the move, and so our history unfolded in Winston-Salem.

Archie looked at Ed for a long time. He said, "We should never have left."

Whether this was a casual remark, designed to honor the past, or a serious wish, neither said. Archie and I often imagined a life in which we would buy the campus and run our own college. Instead, Archie and Ed recalled the memories which remained in place on the old campus.

Two iconic sights at the original Wake Forest College are the brick wall and arch *(above)*

Library Wake Forest College, N. C.

IMAGES THIS PAGE, WAKE FOREST HISTORICAL MUSEUM, WAKE FOREST, NC

: : :

Sometime past midnight, the Hoot Owl, as the night train was called, left Raleigh behind and headed north, with a stop in the sleeping college town of Wake Forest. The sound of the whistle hung in the air for a long time. After a night out in Raleigh, if the boys couldn't thumb a ride back to Wake Forest—which sat smack-dab in the middle of US 1, which ran right up to Faculty Avenue—or they had missed the last Greyhound bus, they could hurry to catch the last train leaving the station.

Wake Forest College did not have a school cafeteria, and students had limited options for their meals. Many paid a fee to eat at a boarding house ($22 a month for three meals a day); others ate at Miss Jo Williams's cafeteria, and some took meals downtown at one of the small cafes. Archie's mother was a good cook, and he hadn't found anything at the college to equal her food. But he made friends with a married ministerial student, and he sometimes bought a steak and took it to their house for his friend's wife to cook for them. He mostly stayed to himself, boarding with the Dickson family on Faculty Avenue. He found the nearby small downtown "rowdy" on a Saturday night, and he was not often one of many students who hitchhiked to the nearby capital of Raleigh, where they ate out and attended games and concerts.

The return to the old campus brought back memories of when Archie and Phyllis began their courtship.

Archie had been studying Spanish with a shipmate in the Navy, and when he enrolled at Wake Forest he signed up for an advanced class with a new teacher, Phyllis Plumbo, who had graduated from Douglass College (the women's college of Rutgers University) and had worked towards her Master's in Spanish at UC-Berkeley, which she had loved. Berkeley, Phyllis said, "opened up the world to me." Her brother was enrolled at Wake Forest and had let her know that they were looking for a Spanish teacher to help teach the large number of students returning from the war. She had come for an interview and was given the job. Within a few months Archie asked her to go out with him. The relationship quickly turned from teacher-student to something else. Archie and Phyllis explored the town together in walks at night on quiet streets with rock walls, magnolia trees, church steeples, and stately brick buildings. Only the sound of the train passing through broke the silence. There were fields and forests to be explored, both for botany classes and on their walks. Archie made his own life.

Faculty homes were another source of entertainment. Faculty members often had students boarding in their homes or invited them for meals, and Archie had been to one of the most culturally sophisticated homes in town—that of Dr. Allen Easley, a Baptist minister and chair of the Religion Department. He and Mrs. Easley had a beautiful camellia garden, where they often held parties. For a voice recital in their home, Archie accompanied two vocalists on the piano. He was given a tour of Dr. Easley's library, where he admired his collection of books about camellias. Archie could not have had a better introduction to an idyllic campus life than here at the Easleys', whose home was filled with lovely antiques, books, friends, and stimulating conversations. It was important enough to him that he described the evening in a letter to Phyllis as one of his examples of what he desired—"a life of beauty."

When Archie asked Miss Plumbo to meet him after class, he had in mind dating her. And she quickly agreed to see him, despite the fact that one of her colleagues said that Ammons was a "wild man." The rumored wildness was quite different from how Archie presented himself as afraid to act on his desire for women because of the teachings of his "pious Christian mother." But the courtship developed quickly. They "walked in the quiet afternoons or sat on the doorsteps of Mrs. Dickson's house and watched the stars come out." Inside the house, they drew the blinds, and they danced. He confessed in his journal that he was "afraid to get closer." He felt that she was "an untouchable" Once, he reminded her, "I touched your hand or you took my arm and we smiled at one another." So they began to walk and to talk and to listen to music, and the courtship caught fire, for both of them. Each desired the other but was afraid of their great differences—he a Southern farm boy, she a daughter of a South Jersey industrialist. They told me in separate conversations that they had never before felt drawn to someone so intensely. He was such a brilliant student in her class that she felt from the beginning that he would be successful at anything he tried. She was glad to hear that he was enjoying his biology classes, however, and encouraged him to become a scientist. When he tried to explain the hold that literature had on him, she felt that there was something "mysterious" about poetry which she could not understand. They continued talking, and unknown to Phyllis, Archie was unclear himself about what being a poet would mean. He was working things out in his mind by talking with her. After Phyllis left at the end of the semester, they continued writing letters and exchanging poems.

: : :

Now, more than 25 years later, back on the old campus where they had met and courted, Archie and Phyllis seemed satisfied with their choices—Phyllis said that Archie's studies at Wake Forest had enabled him to take the next steps, studies at Berkeley, before 12 years of business in New Jersey, and from there in 1964 to Cornell. Taking a chance on returning to North Carolina for a year at Wake Forest was also good thing: they had spent time with his sisters, Mona Ammons Smith and her family, who had moved away but were home for visits, and Vida Ammons Cox and her family, introducing their son John to Vida and Allen Cox's three sons, and revisiting the rural landscapes of Columbus and neighboring Bladen counties.

In January 1992 after a visit with Vida and using our small cottage in Swansboro, close to the White Oak River and beaches at Emerald Isle, Archie and Phyllis drove home to Ithaca. After arriving, he sat down and wrote to me, "We drove back in one day and loved every minute of it. We loved every minute of being in your house with its clusters of invention and composition and memory." Archie had found peace in the land of his birth, and in a pattern of leaving and returning to it.

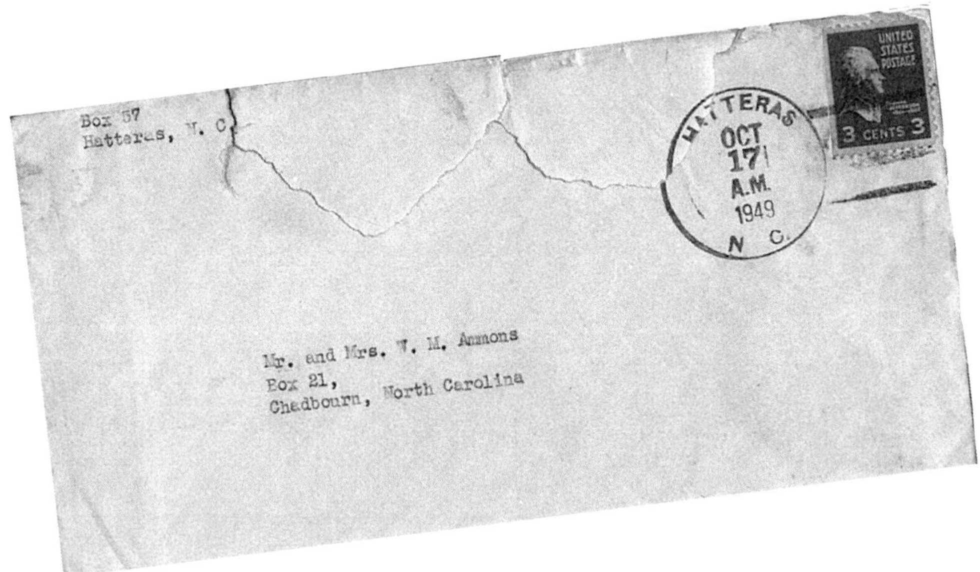

A.R. AMMONS COLLECTION, SPECIAL COLLECTIONS & ARCHIVES, JOYNER LIBRARY, ECU

COURTSEY OF JOHN R. AMMONS

Archie and his son, John Ammons

COURTSEY OF JOHN R. AMMONS

Archie and John Ammons, Christmas, 1967, at the Plumbo home in Northfield, NJ

COURTSEY OF JOHN R. AMMONS

I Was Born in

a poem by **A.R. AMMONS**

I was born in
Whiteville, a southern place: I can
remember when the sidewalks were
planks over muddy holes and when the
stores were tin-roofed shacks; at
least some of them (the stores); then
Leder's was built, a big department
store in the middle of the block;
but not right in
Whiteville: go about a mile on past
Soul's Swamp to South Whiteville south
where the road forks off to New
Brunswick but keep on straight pretty
Soon on a dirt road splits off to the
right: go that way: far aback in
there, after some turnings and
windings, sandhills and branches, you
come around a curve and go up a little
and there is a place, on the right,
the pecan tree and pear tree still
standing: but no house: no mother or
father: just where it all used to be:
isn't that just like life:

Archie on the family farm in Columbus County

"My home country": Columbus County

"Things go away to return, brightened by the passage"
—*from* ***Sphere: The Form of a Motion*** *by* A.R. AMMONS

Where is this place, what Helen Vendler called "the rural hiddenness" of Archie's home country? As Vida observed, when Archie came for a visit, as soon as he said hello, he'd leave her house and he'd go alone to the family cemetery at New Hope Baptist Church, where his parents and young brothers were buried.

WHEN I GO BACK TO MY HOME COUNTRY

At the cemetery he walks among the graves, reading the names of family. He stops at the Ammons marker and the names of his parents:

LUCY DELLA MCKEE AMMONS 1888–1950

WILLIAM M. AMMONS 1895–1966

His long shadow falls across the headstones of

INFANT AMMONS 1922–1923, dead before Archie was born.

INFANT AMMONS 1931, dead at birth.

It is the last stone that most draws him: WILLIE EBERT AMMONS 1928–1930. When his last little brother died, Archie was four years old. Although the cause of his death remains unclear, Archie perhaps harbored guilt that it was his fault—apparently while Archie was supposed to be looking after Ebert, whom he adored, the boy had eaten raw peanuts and got sick and died. It was a grief and a guilt Archie would never get over, and which he memorializes in his poem "Easter Morning":

Willie Ebert Ammons tombstone
photo by Jeffrey Cox, 2019

it is to his grave I most
frequently return and return
to ask what is wrong, what was
wrong, to see it all by
the light of a different necessity
but the grave will not heal
and the child
stirring, must share my grave
with me, an old man having
gotten by on what was left

when I go back to my home country in these
fresh far-away days, it's convenient to visit
everybody, aunts and uncles, those who used to say,
look how he's shooting up, and the
trinket aunts who always had a little
something in their pocketbooks, cinnamon bark
or a penny or nickel, and uncles who
were the rumored fathers of cousins
who whispered of them as of great, if
troubled, presences, and school
teachers, just about everybody older
(and some younger) collected in one place
waiting, particularly, but not for
me, mother and father there, too, and others
close, close as burrowing
under skin, all in the graveyard
assembled, done for, the world they
used to wield, have trouble and joy
in, gone

He returns to his car, and drives away, down a lonely road.

: : :

Columbus remains one of North Carolina's most rural counties, where big cotton and sweet potato farms have displaced the small subsistence farms that failed in the 1930s, when Archie's father gave up and moved to work for his brother John, the sheriff in nearby Whiteville. The county seat, its population today is a little over 5,500, more than twice what it was when Archie attended Whiteville High School, with its social distinction between the town kids and the country ones. Most of the region is forested by loblolly and longleaf pine, the land broken up by lakes and swamps. It still looks isolated. Alligators crawl out of ditches and canals around Lake Waccamaw, and at night scuttling possums crossing roads convey their disdain, turn around and snarl. It's not a place you'd want to be lost in after dark. Flat fields, winding roads, trucks loaded with timber, and the occasional convenience store now and again give way without pronouncement to a row of new two-story brick houses with three-car garages, before giving the past back to small clapboard shacks, sheltered by massive oaks and framed by small family graveyards. After dark, a single light in the back of a house illuminates a kitchen table, where aproned women serve up bowls of mashed potatoes, collards, corn bread, fried fish, and cobblers as good as you'd get, eaten in silence, a family time.

Columbus is the third largest county in North Carolina, in the southernmost part of the state and a couple of hours from Raleigh. North Carolina is divided into three parts—from Raleigh to the Atlantic is the coastal plains; west of Raleigh to Greensboro and Winston-Salem is the piedmont, and on to Hickory, Marion, and Asheville, the mountainous west. History has changed the state's economy: rich planters established the colonial government in the East, before the capital was moved from New Bern to Raleigh; railroads were built, industry brought jobs to the piedmont; and tourism moved to the west. By the time Archie had lived for more than thirty years in New York state, Columbus County was mostly by-passed by families cruising the interstate on the way to their second-homes on beaches around Wilmington; during Archie's day, local families mostly favored the nearby lakes, dark and cold and silent save for the wind, kicking up white waves across their wide expanse. (Archie's grand-niece recently won a contest called Take the Lake, swimming shore to shore at Lake Waccamaw.) Back in the day, sometimes Archie's family would load up with others in the community to travel most of the day on a flat-top model-T thirty miles over oyster shell roads to Cherry Grove Beach, just over the South Carolina state border, to what's now North Myrtle Beach.

On Lake Waccamaw at Dale's Seafood Restaurant oyster roasts are popular. Less private than Lake Waccamaw, where there are no commercial beaches, is White Lake in the Bladen Lakes State Park, some 30 miles north of Whiteville, where trailer parks are popular and families have built homes along the shore. Many local landowners did well, and families (and churches) took pride in belonging to small eastern North Carolina towns. Vida's son Johnny, who operates a large farming operation, and his wife JoAnn, a retired teacher still active in the community, have a charming cottage on Lake Waccamaw, where Vida enjoys taking visitors. But other children and grandchildren grew up and went away, and a few old family houses are kept up, and some fall down. Small towns like Clarkton were popular for visiting and shopping, when after harvest season farmers brought their families to town and the women had money to buy annual school clothes for their children. But downtown Clarkton, Vida's home, now has empty storefronts, except for the historic hardware store—a treasure trove of everything you'd need, including seasonal plants— and the new Family Dollar; some outsider has bought one of the old houses and is fixing it up. At the edge of town is a large peanut plant (owned by a Cox relative), where Vida orders cans of roasted peanuts for our Christmas presents. We send her Mrs. Hanes' Moravian Cookies from Winston-Salem. The single traffic light changes, a few cars move on. Tomorrow the congregation at the lovely Presbyterian Church will be small, but there will be Vida and her son Johnny and his wife and a few newer members—who adapt to visiting ministers, and who always will show up with a casserole when there's a death in a family. There is a deep, deep loyalty to place among the old-timers.

Archie Ammons took pride in Columbus County, and Columbus County takes pride in Archie: the 25th anniversary of the A.R. Ammons Poetry Competition for students has just been celebrated. At the only high school reunion he ever attended, he was wary of meeting his old classmates, some of the townies who had made him feel inferior as one of the country boys. But when he read his poems at the Southeastern Community College in Whiteville, lines formed for him to autograph books. He was a smiling man that day, and his people were proud to bring him home.

Five Poems

by A.R. AMMONS

WHEN I GO BACK
TO MY
HOME COUNTRY

I Went Back

I went back
to my old home
and the furrow
of each year
plowed like
surf across
the place had
not washed
memory away.

Chiseled Clouds

A single
cemetery
wipes out
most
of my
people,
skinny old
slabs
leaning this
way and that
as in stray winds,
holding names:

Still, enough
silver
cathedrals fill
this
afternoon sky
to
house everyone
ever
lost from
the
light's returning.

Father

I dreamed my father flicked
in his grave
then like a fish in water
wrestled with the ground
surfaced and wandered:
I could not find him
through woods, roots, mires
in his bad shape: and
when I found him he was
dead again and had to be
re-entered in the ground:
I said to my mother I still
have you, but out of the
dream I know she died
sixteen years before his
first death:
as I became a child again
a longing that will go away
only with my going grows.

Motioning

My father did not
get a resolution
to his problems: he

was taken down
from them: a
vessel broke

in his brain, and
he lost half his
capability: he

walked less and
asked no questions:
sense returned

to his eyes and
with one hand he held
the other

up: that was
stopped when the
central

heart, of which there
is only one
ticked off: my

father, I could
tell, had
a lot of questions to

ask: but all
motion was
removed from the matter.

My Father, I Hollow for You

My father, I hollow for you
  in the ditches
O my father, I say,
and when brook light, mirrored,
worms
  against the stone ledges
  I think it an unveiling
or coming loose, unsheathing
of flies
O apparition, I cry,
  you have entered in
  and how may you come
  out again
  your teeth will not
  root
  your eyes cannot
unwrinkle, your handbones
may not quiver and stir
O, my father, I cry,
are you returning:
I breathe and see:
it is not you yet it is you

PHOTOGRAPHIC ARCHIVES, NC COLLECTION, WILSON LIBRARY, UNC-CH

Pleasant Grove Cemetery, Ithaca, NY
photo by Emily Herring Wilson

Daytrip to Columbus County

As I toss out a barrage of questions from the passenger's seat of Archie's Chevrolet, he hunches over the wheel, scowls, and slows down to a crawl on a narrow back-country road near the old home place, a few miles from the small village of Chadbourn. He hesitates, then stops but does not cut the engine and gestures out his window toward a stand of scraggly pines, meaning, there it is. On this early spring morning in 1976, Archie is giving me a quick tour of what in poems he has called his "home country." He and Phyllis and Ed and I have driven from Winston-Salem. Phyllis is a quiet rider in the back seat with Ed, and Archie does most of the talking. In our three-hour drive, we have been talking about Columbus County. This morning I have been waiting anxiously for this moment to see the 50 backwoods acres his father owned, 15 of them for crops, where as a boy Archie plowed with the mules Kate and Silver, tenderly described in poems, and to walk into the house where he was born, also recorded in verse as being in the room in the northwest corner. But there is no break in the trees and underbrush nor a house in sight. All that remains are two pecan trees and a pear tree. The house is gone.

Archie puts the car in gear and steps on the gas, and before I know it, we are out of there. He says nothing and color drains from his face. As we drive away, Archie is very quiet, but once we are back in Whiteville, he takes a sudden turn in the downtown and stops in front of a well-maintained classic brick school building that announces "Whiteville High School." He says, "My teacher saw that I had talent. We still keep in touch." (In a 1951 journal entry titled "Snatches from a Portrait," he identifies her as Ruth M. Baldwin, who "taught me English in the 8th and 11th grades. She knew how to teach English so that no one could resist learning it; she actually made it interesting and exciting.")

And then he drives on, the mood lighter, and soon we are on the way back to Winston-Salem, and Archie drives fast.

COURTSEY OF JOHN R. AMMONS

606 Hanshaw Road, the Ammons home in Ithaca, 1966–1992, until they moved to nearby Cayuga Heights Road

Beginning an Epic

a poem by EMILY HERRING WILSON

The place had not been defined
for him when he came to teach.

Hot, an August afternoon, lost
on the nameless roads, looking

for home. That he would come to
sleep and wake here for a time,

seemed only something he dreamed,
far away, in some other body.

Now the fruits of his dreaming
grow in the green fields and

his care is known even by
the insects. The idols that small

men made grew dusty and fell
down; and he stayed in the

shadows, until time to sit down,
to listen, then to speak.

His quiet voice sounds the
intensity of our need, and will

echo in the rooms and out in the
open when he is gone. Like

warriors who travel long
and far in search of the great

task, may he travel back to
this place, defined by his absence.

Sabbatical, part 4

"The longest thing in Winston-Salem is Sunday morning"
—*from* ***"Summer Place"*** *by* A.R. AMMONS

Archie's sabbatical at Wake Forest had created a busy year for the family: John, who spent his third-grade year in Winston-Salem, remembers "the throng of kids who were seemingly all my age that lived on the block. It was through the kids that I discovered football and basketball. I think I'd been overly sheltered in Ithaca!" Phyllis found things she hadn't expected (farmers markets, fine grocery stores, estate sales), and Archie had neighbors and colleagues to talk to at every turn. I spent part of every day with Phyllis (she taught me to be a careful shopper), and with Archie I read poetry, gossiped, and argued about money—he saved, I spent. John was entertained many Saturday mornings in our living room, where Ed read *The Hardy Boys* to John and Eddie and their friends, sprawled on the couches and leaving a trail of cookie crumbs when they bolted as the last chapter was finished and raced to play in the creek that ran behind John's house and ours.

Then, all too soon, the year was over. Archie, Phyllis, and John left Winston-Salem early on a Saturday morning at the end of May in 1975 and headed north, to spend the summer in Ocean City, New Jersey, close to Phyllis's family and where she and Archie had lived with her parents when they returned from Archie's graduate studies at Berkeley. Archie and Phyllis had often walked the New Jersey shore, and he wrote some of his best poems there. "Corsons Inlet" was one of them. This time he wrote a long poem, more than 1,000 lines, 45 pages, "Summer Place," which included some description of his time in North Carolina and life on Royall Drive in the faculty neighborhood. It's a complaining poem—people ask too much of him, he doesn't like certain kinds of poets and poems; Sunday in Winston-Salem is the longest day of the year. He was not to publish "Summer Place" until 1996, in *Brink Road*. Maybe he was afraid that he had been too critical, and his peevishness had passed. When I read it, I wondered if his querulousness had anything to do with Winston-Salem, but I didn't take it personally. I had learned early in our friendship that Archie answered only to Archie.

All that summer we wrote or called to say we missed one another and tried to find things of interest to report. John enjoyed the South

Jersey beaches, Phyllis spent time with her family, and Archie made friends at "a poetry fling" at the local cultural center. But something was unsettled—as expressed in "Summer Place." It is not unusual for one to feel at sixes and sevens after having completed some kind of purposeful enterprise; so perhaps it was to be expected that, in leaving North Carolina behind, Archie would experience a new set of annoyances, or "sizzling" angers, as he suggests. He did not have enough to do to distract him—Phyllis with her family, John with his cousins, families on the beaches—faculty lounge confabs at Wake Forest behind him and the Cornell Temple of Zeus mornings distantly remote. As he wrote me on a Sunday morning from Ocean City, when Phyllis and John had gone to Northfield to see her family, "I think I am really tired of poetry for a while but unable to find anything else entertaining, a mess." Archie often insisted he wasn't writing anymore, but he was very good at thinking up new projects, and by the end of the summer when they left New Jersey behind and returned to Ithaca, he had a new idea.

Moving back into their house on Hanshaw Road, Archie set up a table in the upstairs bedroom looking out into the backyard he loved so much and had written about so often, and he began painting watercolors. In 1977 he was painting as many as six or eight hours a day. In 1981, he described the process in one of the most revealing statements he ever made about the sources of his creativity:

> There is a poetics of tears, of smiles, of ecstasy (sensual joy and the harsh inspirations of the religious heights); there is a poetics of quietude and deep study, a poetics of fear—and a poetics of anger.
>
> During Christmas vacation in 1976, I got the notion, which I had had passingly but often before, to try watercolors. I'm sure I was attracted to the possibility of bringing together in one visual consideration the arbitrariness of pure coincidence with the necessity of the essential, the

**New Hope
Baptist Church
cemetery, 2019**
photo by Diane Vitale

> moving from the free, as the work of art begins, through the decisions of pattern and possibility, and into and through the demands of the necessary, the unavoidable, the inevitable. This "change" is in another form the oldest of journeys, that from exile to community.
>
> Having had dozens of tries at real pictures, I began to feel what events on the paper "meant"—that is, I began to learn the joining of what happened on the paper to its emotional counterpart, the feelings generated and expressed by the events. I discovered that I was stirred by the thin, loud, and bright, the utterly blatant effect like a smack in the face, the anger felt, expressed, reacted to. And then I thought that not a very nice thing to be into. But I was angry, sizzlingly angry for whatever reasons, and I found myself, when I could endure the emotions at all, released by letting the anger go and become the splatters and the sheer control of the paint. And then I thought that since we must after all at times be angry, how fortunate we are that art allows us to transform blistering feelings into the brilliance, the sweep and curve, the dash and astonishment (along with the cool definition, judgment, and knowledge) of still completed things.

Because painting the watercolors became a daily effort not long after his sabbatical year at Wake Forest, I have wondered what happened to ignite such an explosion of pictures—what made him so "sizzlingly angry"—mostly the pictures are abstract expressionist. Art critics have told me that they are exceptional.

Friends for Life

After the 1974–75 sabbatical, the Ammonses and the Wilsons had become friends for life, and there would be many shorter visits over the next 25 years, sometimes for Archie to visit family and friends, sometimes to teach workshops and classes at Wake Forest, sometimes to vacation on the North Carolina coast, and sometimes the Wilsons drove to Ithaca and vacationed in the Finger Lakes region. Archie wrote Ed expressing his gratitude, Ed responded with gratitude for himself and for the University; and Phyllis and I wrote or called, remembering our good times. We all had to adjust to the change from having seen one another almost every day—John and Eddie missed the gang; they were each other's first best friend—and I had no one to turn to without Phyllis to advise me about cooking and decorating and a thousand common sense ideas about how to make life more beautiful—she would have been great on *Antiques Roadshow*, she had such an eye for quality. Archie wrote postcards and wrote letters on half-sheets of Cornell stationery and sometimes longer letters of several pages. I typed long letters, full of effusive love and news about the family and friends they had made here.

And so our lives continued. Archie, who said he could not write any more poems, wrote more poems, and more books were published: *Diversifications* in 1975; his second *Selected Poems*, *Highgate Road* and *The Snow Poems* in 1977; the *Selected Longer Poems 1951-1977* in 1978; *A Coast of Trees* in 1981; *Worldly Hopes* in 1982; *Lake Effect Country* in 1983; *Sumerian Vistas* in 1987; *The Really Short Poems* in 1991; *Garbage* in 1993; *The North Carolina Poems* in 1994; *Brink Road* in 1996; and *Glare* in 1997. Others would be published posthumously: *Bosh and Flapdoodle* in 2005; yet another *Selected Poems* in 2006; an expanded edition of *The North Carolina Poems* and *The Mule Poems* in 2010; and, finally, in two fat volumes *The Complete Poems* in 2017.

And the prizes with his name on them piled up: the Bollingen Prize for *Sphere*, the National Book Critics Circle Award for *A Coast of Trees*; a second National Book Award, for *Garbage*; the inaugural Wallace Stevens Award in 1981; the Robert Frost Medal and Ruth Lilly Prize and fellowships from the Guggenheim Foundation and the American Academy of Arts and Letters. He was elected a Fellow of the American Academy of Arts and Letters in 1978 and inducted into the North Carolina Literary Hall of Fame in 2000, just a few months before he died.

Since self-publishing *Ommateum* in 1955, Archie had written nearly thirty books. As he continued to publish after his Wake Forest sabbatical, he sent autographed copies to us and our children, and we gave copies to friends. The homecoming of A.R. Ammons for his Wake Forest sabbatical had not just changed our lives, it changed our reading habits. Now we were all reading Ammons. The more we read, the more we understood, until I began to believe that his poetry could be read by every "amateur reader." I took every invitation that came my way to discuss his poetry with book clubs, classes, and libraries, and slowly I began to see that there were many Ammons poems that readers found accessible. They chose their favorites.

I continued to write poems and to send them to Archie and to have them accepted by chapbook publishers, but I had begun to lose interest in writing poetry, and my attention was turning toward nonfiction, especially women's biographies, and community activism. I began traveling all over the state, interviewing subjects for two books: *For the People of North Carolina, a History of the Z. Smith Reynolds Foundation*, published in 1988, and then *Hope and Dignity: Older Black Women of the South*, published in 1992. Archie was generous in his praise of both, taking copies to his office to pass around to his faculty friends, especially recommending a chapter in *For the People* about the decline of a small town, Gibson, North Carolina, which surely reminded him of his birthplace.

Ed and I and our children were also traveling: we spent Ed's sabbatical near Boston and we drove cross-country to California. I taught workshops in writing and reading poetry and in conducting oral histories and was active on many boards supporting literature, race relations, and public education. I taught classes at Salem College, including one which included Ammons in contemporary poetry, and I organized public lectures and seminars in women's journal writing and took assignments as a visiting artist in state community colleges. Archie showed little interest in my community affairs and no interest in my politics. He admired my values, said he couldn't survive a day of my appointments, but he always asked about friends at Wake Forest. And he was glad that we kept up with his sister Vida. She came to Winston-Salem to visit us and we went to Clarkton to see her. We talked often on the phone with her, as she did with Archie.

Meanwhile, Archie, too, was staying busy.

After returning to Cornell from Wake Forest, he seemed to have renewed energy. From the first of September 1976 to the end of May in 1977 during the longest, coldest winter in American history, he made a long poem out of daily observations about the weather and life in Ithaca. Archie loved the Ithaca winters, and he especially loved the snow (there had been two dustings of snow during their year in North Carolina), and the snow, I think, was an important reason he preferred Ithaca to Winston-Salem. He often said that *The Snow Poems*, one long poem, was his favorite book, though the book received some harsh reviews (Archie often liked his poems that critics were hardest on. He told me and others in his workshops, "If someone tells you not to do something, do it again. You will find your true voice.") During the same period, he continued painting watercolors and stacked them up. Sometimes he sold one or two when someone asked, and on occasion he showed some in a gallery in Ithaca, and he brought some to North Carolina and sold them. He loved selling a painting, even for as little as $30.

REYNOLDA HOUSE MUSEUM OF AMERICAN ART, WINSTON-SALEM

Maya Angelou joined the Wake Forest University faculty as Reynolds Professor of American Studies in 1982. She and Archie met at Reynolda House Museum of American Art, where each read poetry on special occasions.
photo by Susan Mullally, about 1986

Ticks and Teeth

In 1980 at the invitation of Nick Bragg, Archie and Phyllis and John returned to the South for Archie to teach a writing workshop in rural Virginia, at a place called Critz, the birthplace of R.J. Reynolds, in a learning center directed by Virginia Tech University. They lived in an upstairs apartment in an 1810 historic house and had a good time trying out country living. Nick himself assembled twenty beds for the participants in the program and had showers installed and meals catered in the education building. In all these ways Archie was impressed that his Wake Forest friends would go to any extent to accommodate his needs. Eddie and John renewed their friendship. Among the participants that hot summer were Kay Stripling Byer, who would become North Carolina's seventh Poet Laureate, and Michael McFee, who has since published many collections of poetry and still teaches creative writing at the University of North Carolina at Chapel Hill.

The heat that summer was fierce, and Archie warned everyone to look out for ticks, and he complained that he had taught more those two weeks than he did in a semester at Cornell. I remember it as one of the times Archie was having the most fun. I love recalling his happy laughter. He agreed to come back the following summer, when the two-week poetry workshop would be in Winston-Salem, at Reynolda House, which would also present an exhibition of Archie's watercolors. The heat and the ticks of the country had convinced him that the lakeside porch at Reynolda House would be the better setting. Nick put Archie and Phyllis up in the second floor rooms at Reynolda House, where Archie's sisters also stayed when they came.

Nick's favorite story from that summer is that one early morning when he was coming to work he saw someone walking toward him, "a pink apparition." It was Archie, backlit by the early morning sun.

"Let's go to breakfast," Archie said.

"Of course," Nick agreed. "Where do you want to go"?

Archie said, "Howard Johnson's, because they have soft biscuits that don't hurt my teeth." And off they went.

Nick follows this story with another: it was Christmas Eve, the house about ready to close up to visitors for the holidays, when he heard someone shout, "Mabel, come look at this!" He went downstairs and found a husband and his wife wandering through. He welcomed them, and they said they were on their way from Ithaca, New York, to Florida and had stopped to see Reynolda House.

"Well," Nick said. "I have a great friend from Ithaca who stayed right in this house. I took him to breakfast at Howard Johnson's because he said he had bad teeth and the soft biscuits were easy to chew."

The man laughed and said, "Well, I'm Archie's dentist, and I pulled his teeth! He was the one who told me to come by to see Reynolda House. So here we are!"

No

In spring 1983, I went to Cornell bearing a verbal invitation to Archie from my husband, Ed, to consider returning to teach in the Wake Forest Department of English on whatever basis he might choose. Ed was not sure what would be most attractive to Archie on another short-term or long-term affiliation, and trusting our friendship he had wanted me to explore possibilities with him with my show of willingness to fly to Ithaca and give Archie and Phyllis a chance to talk about what might appeal to them.

But from the minute I was met at the airport and taken to their house on Hanshaw Road, I was uneasy. Archie in person seemed less friendly and approachable than Archie in letters and on the phone. Phyllis settled me into the upstairs guest room, and I did not linger but immediately came downstairs. I wanted to get it over with: the business I had come to transact.

But no sooner had we finished another of Phyllis's great meals and I had begun to talk to Archie about Wake Forest did I realize that it had all been a mistake. Archie began at once to lay out the reasons why he would not accept a permanent job offer from Wake Forest. He paced back and forth and refused to look at me. He would never consider leaving Cornell. He had everything at Cornell. Wake Forest had nothing to offer him that he didn't already have.

I was stunned.

Archie left the room.

Phyllis was embarrassed, I was alarmed, and the evening ended quickly with my going upstairs to my room. The house was small enough that we could hear one another moving about, which I think was part of the problem for Archie, and I was eager to go to bed. The next morning everyone was quiet, Archie and I went over to the Temple of Zeus, but I left soon and met Phyllis for shopping, and we had easy conversations. She took me to the airport, saying very little, and I left, shaken and confused.

I wrote immediately to thank Archie for having had me as a guest, apologizing if I had intruded in any way, and hoping we could take up where we had left off before my disastrous trip—and that we still had a friendship we could count on. I received this letter from him, written by hand on a half-sheet of Cornell stationery.

> 7 April '83
> Dear Emily,
> Your beautiful letter has made us feel so good. I'm glad you're not mad with me. You did your work here so well and you were so delightful to have here that the best I could have done was accept any offer you made. I'm stuck with myself right now & can't budge. It isn't Wake Forest.
>
> Thanks for all the news—and of Eddie's recovery [Eddie had been home with pneumonia]. Our love to the girls and to all—Archie.

(In a postcard Archie had written me a decade earlier, in 1973 when he was seriously considering taking Robert Penn Warren's place at Yale, he confessed about the possibility of moving, "Makes me shake in the shanks." He didn't go to Yale. In other words, leaving Cornell was a BIG DEAL, as Archie might have put it in a poem.)

: : :

This experience continued to weigh on me in ways that made me uncertain for a long time about how to approach him. I knew that increasingly he did not like to be asked to do anything for anybody. He felt overwhelmed—especially by unsolicited poetry manuscripts that came in the mail and by requests for recommendations.

In time, things returned to what seemed normal—conversations about our lives, frequent contact in calls and letters. Phyllis and Archie did return to Wake Forest on a number of occasions, and all seemed well. But what had set him off that awful evening on Hanshaw Road? He never again spoke directly of any of this to me, but his contacts with Ed suddenly turned affectionate and frequent.

Not long after my visit to Ithaca, Archie wrote Ed at the Provost's office to say that he was mailing him a book. This was not a surprise because Archie had written Ed the year before to say that he wanted to dedicate his next book, *Lake Effect Country*, to him. The dedication would say "For Edwin G. Wilson, friend's friend, Archie," and, he wrote, "I do offer it in the clearest hope that you will accept, for we go back so far your acceptance would open one of negotiation's longest avenues."

28 May '83

Dear Ed,

Just a note to say I'm having a copy of *Lake Effect Country* sent you directly. I hope someday to sign it for you. But if I don't, I'll send you a signed copy from here later.

The dedication distresses me. [Someone might have] thought it meant "friend of a friend" but I meant it the same as poet's poet—friend's friend—you the finest example of that all around. I'm sorry.

I'm going to write you about your letter someday [inviting him to join the Wake Forest faculty]. I can't come. I'm under a lot of tension, which has been hypertension & which I'm finding it difficult to treat. WFU has all the natural attachments for me, but I have so little strength for change these days.

Love to the family. I hope Emily is not completely cutting her ties with us. She was so noble & warm when here.
Love, Archie

UNIVERSITY SPECIAL COLLECTIONS & ARCHIVES, Z. SMITH REYNOLDS LIBRARY, WAKE FOREST UNIVERSITY

Ed Wilson, center, with Wake Forest singers

Wake Forest, 1986

"It is my place where / I must stand or fall"
—*from* ***"Easter Morning"*** *by* A.R. AMMONS

In 1986 Archie returned to Wake Forest again when we celebrated his 60th birthday and invited Helen Vendler as the keynote speaker. I was then teaching poetry at Salem College. Archie visited my classes, and I directed an Ammons seminar, sponsored by the North Carolina Humanities Council. Archie was nervous, wanting to back out, but finally agreed to go through with the weekend. Helen was magnificent, and the highlight was her reading of "Easter Morning," a poem which she called "sublime," and which indeed had become one of many readers' favorite Ammons poems.

We should have stopped with Helen's talk and proceeded with Archie and Phyllis and Vida to the president's house for the birthday party, but we had invited other guests, notably Wayne Pond, from the National Humanities Center, who was to interview Archie on stage. But from the time Pond asked the first question, things didn't go well. Archie was overcome with stage fright, and I stepped in to help. Together Wayne and I guided him through a few questions, accepted his short answers, and brought things to a merciful close.

By the time we gathered for birthday cake, Archie had relaxed, talking to his sister Vida. And all that anyone could remember was Helen's reading of "Easter Morning." Archie told me that his student and friend, Jerald Bullis, whose long poem *Orion* we had published with Jackpine Press in 1976, had urged Archie to take "Easter Morning" out of a much longer poem called "Improvisation for the Other Way Around," drafted in 1977, and publish it as a stand-alone poem, and Archie had agreed. Even great poets can learn from their students.

Participants were given copies of "Easter Morning," handset in an elegant booklet by designer Richard Murdoch and a treasure, if it can still be found. Alice Barkley, director of the N.C. Humanities Council, who staged the birthday celebration with such success that the NCHC has never had another seminar that so closely matched a great scholar and a great poet to a public audience. That was Archie's great gift—to leave us something to live by. I don't think I've ever been part of any literary occasions in which love of words and one another so lit up our lives. As I remember this occasion 35 years later, I can still see the poet, smiling.

It was over, and he felt okay.

Ed Wilson's senior portrait, Wake Forest College, from *The Howler*, 1943

Ed Wilson at work as editor of *The Howler*, 1943, at Wake Forest College

PHOTOS THIS PAGE, SPECIAL COLLECTIONS & ARCHIVES, Z. SMITH REYNOLDS LIBRARY, WAKE FOREST UNIVERSITY

More Friends

Archie made and kept friends easily. When a friendship ended, he seemed mystified, as hurt as any child who has been ignored on the playground or has been publicly reprimanded. I can think of several people who were close to Archie, and then something was said or done that, in a manner of speaking, came between them, and the closeness was broken. He might begin by mentioning it to me, but he would never finish telling me what happened, if he knew, and sometimes I observed a difference on my own. It was not my business to ask who or what or when; so I'm not in the business of speculating now. But I mention broken friendships because I think Archie was capable of being hurt and hurting others, and that is evidence of how important friends were. What I can speak to, however, is his gift for friendships, and I chose three of his friends here because I think they illustrate what a capacity Archie had for feelings about other human beings. I have asked the three to speak for themselves: Shelby Stephenson and Ken Frazelle, who met Archie in North Carolina and maintained their connections to the end of Archie's life; and Ken McClane, who had been one of his MFA students at Cornell and then became a colleague there.

Shelby Stephenson, whom my husband and I have known most of our literary lives, is perhaps the most loved writer on the North Carolina literary scene. With his wife, Nin, he always shows up, always smiling, singing, reading, loving, and he has been rewarded for his talent and dedication to poetry and fellow poets by being selected as North Carolina's eighth Poet Laureate. He would have been the Most Popular Boy in high school; he's our Most Popular Poet now. It is impossible not to love Shelby Stephenson. We had been hoping that he would be named Laureate by the Governor and sooner or later someone in state government got the message that there was a red-headed fellow from eastern North Carolina who knew barbecue and bluegrass, a teacher, a writer, a friend. In 1988 Shelby also edited a special issue of *Pembroke Magazine* on A.R. Ammons, with new poems by Archie. But here is an email to me I want to share. I had asked Shelby if he remembered the night he and Nin were at our house after a Wake Forest Ammons seminar, this one in 1995, and this is what he wrote:

: a remembrance of Archie Ammons :

photo by Susan Mullally, Critz, VA, 1980

COURTSEY OF JOHN R. AMMONS

Archie in the great room in the Cayuga Heights Road home, where he and Phyllis moved from Hanshaw Road in 1992.

May 2, 2008
Dear Emily,
Oh I remember that night.

Archie sat down at the piano. Archie looked at me and asked me if I knew "The Royal Telephone." I said I knew the chorus. He played the song: "Central's never busy, always on the line;

You may hear from heaven almost any time;
'tis a royal service, free for one and all;
when you get in trouble, give this royal line a call."

My brother Paul, the Barbe-Q brother, knew it: Paul was born in '28, Archie in '26. I had heard Paul sing it.

I asked Vida if Archie took piano lessons. She said, "Yes, he rode his bicycle to the lessons."

That may be the night he played "How Great Thou Art." I cannot remember.

What does this have to do with his writing? Music. I can hear the music in his lines.

Another memory: I hooded Archie for the honorary doctorate at UNC-Pembroke, sometime after Nin and I moved from Southern Pines to the home place near the barbecue place where I am typing this to you. We moved back here in spring, '96. I drove into Pembroke [to teach], 80 miles, though I never told anyone that's how far school was from here.

Archie was waiting, a little nervous, already in his robe, when I entered the room with all the "stage" people. (By the way: the microphone was not working in the gymnasium. No one could hear Archie read his poem. And he and Phyllis left soon thereafter. Archie wrote me that he had the budgies. Said he loved the ritual of the ceremony.)

Oh, as I approached him in the room filled with the stage-people he started singing "One Step More." Do you know that song: "One step more from earth to heaven; then we'll reach that other shore"? Something like that.

There are snips and tones of hymns in all his writing. Vida took me to that church he grew up in: Spring Branch. You must know the exact name. [Spring Branch Fire-Baptized Pentecostal Church.] I have heard him say: swell the pulpit. He did that. The music of the sermon and the going on and on all in his work.

Another memory: when he came to Pembroke for the first time. He said he went to Maxton first. And when he arrived, I met him for the first time and he said, "Lord, I could be your uncle." [Grace Gibson took that workshop in the early '80s at Wake Forest and she wrote me a card. She said she told Shelby, "Archie could be your uncle." His red hair scattered on his head.]

One of his students was an Ambrose, Steven Ambrose. He had a copy of *Middle Creek Poems*, my first little book, came out in '79. And Steven took it to a class Archie was teaching.

That's how Archie knew of me. The Ambroses were neighbors of Nin's parents when they lived south of Buffalo, in Boston, NY.

One regret: when we parked our Class B Motorhome out in front of your house, Ed giving me that long orange cord to plug in to your house: Archie got up early one morning and came by the van and did not wake us up. He was going for a walk. I am sorry I missed walking with him.

Oh I can hear the Southerness in the voice in all his work. A little like the going-on-ness in Faulkner. *Go Down, Moses*, *Absalom, Absalom*!

Some of those early poems I love and I keep coming back to them:

"Silver"—the mule poem to end all mule poems. (We had two mules when I was growing up: Black and Gray. Archie's poem, wow, the music, the detail.)

"Hardweed Path Going." Oh I won't forget the jo-reet, Sparkle, his pet pig. Slops not quite spilling over the brim. (I grew up like that too.)

"Nelly Myers," my favorite, if I have to name one. I asked him one time if that was her name. He said, no, her name was Sally Tyree. (Perhaps he thought somehow Sally Tyree might see the poem?)

My dominant image of Archie: always wanting to stay put somewhere and yet not at home anywhere. There was a time he thought he would retire to Southern Pines. Nin and I lived there for 18 years. He drove through it one day and said he did not want to pursue the idea anymore.

I remember the time he had a showing of some paintings at the Morehead Planetarium. I remember [his sister] Mona telling me, "We were not as poor as Archie makes out we were."

Archie was disappointed that no one, I don't think anyone from the faculty at Chapel Hill came to be with him and us. I enjoyed that day.

I felt very close to him in a real way, Emily, for I knew the area around the New Hope community outside Whiteville. And I worked all those years in Pembroke.

I felt his ill at ease, genuine, wanting to be free.

I also felt his boredom at poetry readings. I remember one of the very few meetings of the Modern Language

for Archie

I Went Back

A. R. Ammons

Kenneth Frazelle

Association I went to, this one in Washington, DC. I thought Archie would get up and leave. He was so uncomfortable.

Anyway: that's enough.

I look forward to reading what you write.

Give my love to Ed. To you, too.
—Shelby

Shelby brings back many memories: Archie said at our house, "When I sit at the piano and play those hymns, it makes me feel at home wherever I am."

Page one of the 5-page composition "I Went Back," by Kenneth Frazelle, based on Archie's poem of the same name

: : :

Another remarkable person who became a close friend of Archie's during his North Carolina visits was the nationally acclaimed composer Kenneth Frazelle, who with his partner, the writer Rick Mashburn, is active in the arts in Winston-Salem. Of all the composers who set Archie's words to music, Archie most preferred Ken's, although he never could bring himself to travel to any of the places where Ken's compositions were performed—Boston, New York City, Los Angeles.

Winston-Salem calls itself the City of the Arts, a title that is enhanced by the presence of the University of North Carolina School of the Arts. One of its graduates and a faculty member in composition is Kenneth Frazelle, who having heard Archie read at Wake Forest sat in on one of his writing workshops at Reynolda House in 1981. Ken began writing compositions based on Archie's poems, and although Archie was skeptical at first—he said he had already set his poems to music—he admired the scores that Ken sent him and the two became close friends. Today we hear how close Ken and Archie were alike in their sensibilities when a critic notes that Frazelle's original compositions are "rooted in the folk melodies of his native North Carolina. But like Bartok and Copland his work finally transcends its simple sources to become high art." Archie said of Ken's work, "The range of his invention and technical brilliance is apparently inexhaustible and is accompanied by a profound depth of song or feeling. The poise of that kind of forwarding can produce the highest sense of aesthetic completion."

Archie and Ken, who were distantly kin in eastern North Carolina, came from different backgrounds. Archie's home contained only the Bible and a few pages torn out of *Robinson Crusoe* (for no reason Archie could remember). Ken, on the other hand, although from a family of modest means—his father died when Ken was six—was encouraged from the very beginning by his mother. In high school, his teacher, Gladys Sylvester, the sister of Paul Green, a successful playwright and son of a cultured eastern North Carolina family, prepared him to apply to the newly created state School of the Arts, where he auditioned and was accepted. After graduating, he studied at the Juilliard School, and for over thirty years he has moved gracefully through a succession of stages that have landed him commissions from Berkeley to Boston. Along the way, he set many of Archie's poems to music, performed many places. Each time Archie hoped to attend, but, of course, he backed out at the last minute. (In a letter to Ken in March 1980 Archie explained his reluctance to attend concerts and readings: "I might come to you provided I don't have to do anything before the public & don't have to sit in the midst of the spiral during the performance, I like to hear things from the periphery.")

But he and Ken kept up a lively correspondence after Archie returned to Ithaca: here is Archie's note to Ken about his composition of "Small Song."

> Valentine's '85
> Your piece gives the wind away at that high point just right—and then lets the music itself subside. The rhythm is shocking and beautiful. You are a master.
> Be good now.

COURTESY OF PHIL ARCHER AND REYNOLDA HOUSE MUSEUM OF AMERICAN ART ESTATE ARCHIVES.

Archie relaxes with Ken Frazelle, Winston-Salem resident and nationally known composer. Ken took a poetry writing workshop with Archie in the summer of 1981 at Reynolda House Museum of American Art, where they sit on the lake porch.

: : :

I got to know Ken McClane, poet and essayist and a member of the Cornell writing faculty, when I invited him to come to be on programs honoring Archie here at Wake Forest and later when I taught for a semester at Cornell. I knew how much he and Archie loved one another. And I saw that love at Cornell, when Ken and his beautiful wife, Rochelle, became my best friends, too. No one at Cornell was more welcoming to me than Ken and Rochelle, and I have talked with Ken many times since Archie died, just to get my bearings on what's happening in today's divided America. We are both involved public advocates: Ken is conducting an on-site visitation to an upstate New York prison, an important fact-finding project to refigure New York's prison environment. And I am writing a tribute to public schools in our city. When I visited Phyllis, after Archie died, Ken and Rochelle were the friends she wanted to take out to dinner with me.

There is, however, a missing chapter on my overview of Archie's Cornell years. I am mostly ignorant about the difficult years in the late 1960s and early '70s when race protests disrupted the Cornell campus, and in 1969 students took over Willard Straight Hall, the student union. A much repeated photograph showed students emerging from the building with guns, which brought a new level of potential violence to the race protests of those years. Faculty members were deeply disturbed and divided. Students were entering unknown territory. Archie was frightened, but he was not the only one. As an African-American student, Ken was caught up in the rightness of the need to break down divisions at Cornell. His need brought him into mostly unspoken conflict with Archie, who wanted both to love and support him and to put some distance between himself and the potential for violence. Conflict always stirred up Archie's anxieties: he was afraid. At any rate, it was a hard time at Cornell—its president resigned—and four decades later, campus publications report that the history is not forgotten. But it is a chapter in Cornell's history which I do not know well, and I have asked Ken McClane to write about his friendship with Archie:

I had a special relationship with Archie—he trusted me, and I trusted him. We were of different ages, races, and backgrounds, but we were fellow Romantics, and we always spoke the truth to each other, even if it, at times, caused us to keep our own counsel—to lick our proverbial wounds. Still, when things truly mattered, Archie would provide me with unflinching wisdom. When my brother died of alcoholism, it was Archie who wrote me and called it "unspeakable." When he was asked to teach at Yale, Archie asked me—then an undergraduate—what I thought about his going there. He wanted my advice, because he felt I knew something about those Easterners. I, like him, was an outsider/ insider, and he knew that such a predicament taught one much. But it was often in the seemingly smallest utterance where Archie shared his greatest acumen. "Ken, I'm now sixty but I have the same insecurities I had when I was twelve," he told me one day when I was in my usual state of undergraduate angst. Here, again, Archie was letting me see beyond the curtain, speaking those irrefutable truths that so generously suffuse his poems.

Archie never lied to me, and when we differed, we differed powerfully. But it was a real connection—one that sometimes drew blood but always, in the end, provided healing. I, thanks to him, had a bounty of love and support, and how lucky I was. As he once told me, "Claim your element, claim it mightily. In you, there will always be we."

COURTESY EMILY HERRING WILSON

Archie salutes Emily, who's wearing Archie's hat

My Cornell Semester, 1993

On a cold winter's night in North Carolina, I answered a call from Archie inviting me to come to Cornell to teach for the spring semester 1993. I knew at once that he had found another way to thank me for what I had meant to him. And his department must have indulged his choice when he floated my thin resume to fill the need for a visiting writer that year. It was one of the most unexpected—perhaps undeserved—honors of my life.

Our children were in college and Ed was still in the administration at Wake Forest. He and I agreed that it was really the chance of a lifetime for me, and I accepted Archie's invitation at once. It proved to be a memorable semester—in a new clime in which snow was a regular event, seeing Archie and Phyllis almost every day, having two classes of wonderful writing students (not much different from ours at Wake Forest), making friends with writing faculty in the English Department, and exploring the sights around Ithaca. I was headed for an adventure I had never anticipated. The life of a faculty wife and an organizer of events for others had been good enough for me. Now I was to be on the faculty of one of the great universities. I was excited, and I was scared.

So on a January Saturday in 1993 I locked my cross country skis—acquired for an earlier winter's residence at the MacDowell Colony in New Hampshire and since unused—onto the rack on top of my station wagon, and I drove away, spending the night in Carlisle, Pennsylvania, and arriving at 606 Hanshaw Road, Ithaca, New York, the next day. Archie and Phyllis (John was living in California for college) had recently moved to another house nearby, in Cayuga Heights, and had left the one on Hanshaw Road nicely furnished, just for me, it seemed. That night I had the first of many wonderful meals with them in their new home, watching the sun set over Cayuga Lake.

: : :

At Cornell, Archie set me up royally in his house on Hanshaw. He sponsored me in the department, he gave me his books, and he encouraged my teaching. He was my protector.

After years of adjusting, Archie had become perhaps the most beloved professor on campus. Here his poetry mattered, and he was also accessible to everyone and signaled his willingness to welcome friends and strangers. Slowly, his shyness had faded. He could be playful in his conversations in the hall, but he was found most often in the basement coffee shop of Goldwin Smith Hall, a sort of dungeon, dark and with walls lined with plaster cast replicas of the Temple of Zeus sculptures in Olympia. Called the Temple of Zeus, or more informally simply "Zeus," it was a gathering place where lots of people wasted a lot of time. Archie had already done a day's work by the time he arrived at Zeus, where at a long table he religiously held court for at least a couple of hours daily. No one sat at that table that he didn't want there. (In 1994, Roger Gilbert writes, and over Archie's and others' objections, Zeus was "forcibly relocated" to a "much smaller and less atmospheric space," though still in the same building.)

When Archie escorted visitors into his office, his personality belied its plainness—a few books, an ordinary green house plant he hovered over. After *Garbage* won the National Book Award in 1993, he arrived at work to find that pranksters, faculty and students, had covered his office door, at 239 Goldwin Smith, with candy wrappers and scrap paper, an homage to garbage.

But despite my semester at Cornell being Archie's most generous gift to me, I had an experience which echoed the rudeness I had felt ten years earlier, when I flew to Ithaca with that job offer in hand, for Archie to conclude his career at Wake Forest.

I had a call from a student who had graduated from Wake Forest and was teaching at Syracuse. He had heard from Ed that I was at Cornell, and he called to ask if he could come to see me, and, by the way, could I introduce him to A.R. Ammons. I said I'd see what I could arrange, and I called to ask Phyllis. She invited me to bring him over on a Saturday afternoon, and so we went.

When Phyllis welcomed us at the door and invited us into the living room, Archie refused to come out of his study. After a few awkward minutes of conversation with Phyllis, I made noises about leaving, and Archie looked out from his hiding place and glared at me. I passed a book to Phyllis to give to him to sign, he signed it without coming into the room, and the Wake Forest friend and I left. I tried to apologize to the student, equally embarrassed. But I was also very disappointed in Archie, and angry, too.

The next morning, Archie and Phyllis picked me up for our usual Sunday morning brunch in another nearby town. He was driving, I was in the passenger's seat, and Phyllis was in the back. Without looking at me he began to speak:

"Are you always so nice?" he asked.

"I guess so," I said.

"Even when someone interrupts your life at home, uninvited?"

"I try to be," I said.

And he drove on, slowly.

On the way home through country sites and small towns, nobody talked. Then as we passed the remains of an old house, Archie gestured toward a concrete foundation and said, "I've seen that a hundred times and never have known what it was."

I said nothing.

"What was it used for?" he asked.

"I don't know," I said. I really didn't. "Maybe when they cut ice from the ponds in winter they stored it there, and covered it in straw. At some point, maybe it had walls and a roof, or maybe not. Then in the summer they would bring up blocks of ice to the house."

I looked away.

Archie looked amazed.

"How do you know so much?" he asked.

"I don't know," I said. "But you asked me, and I tried to come up with an answer that made sense."

Archie slowed the car almost to a standstill.

"Thank you for that," he said.

"You're welcome," I said.

We had done penance. I had distracted him from his feeling of guilt (if indeed he had it) by giving him something else to talk about, and we moved on.

When we arrived back in Ithaca, Archie said, "Phyllis will want you to come to supper."

Phyllis agreed from the back seat.

"Not tonight," I said. "It has been a long and disturbing day."

I got out without looking back. Only when I was in the house did I hear him drive away.

Archie had been so peevishly rude to my friend, and I brooded. Had I asked too much? Late that night as the moonlight slanted through the window and I heard Archie's owl, I took it as Archie's apology. Perhaps, or maybe not.

Archie was not a man given to apologies, and I tried never again to put myself in a position with him of needing one. Our friendship deepened in ways that occur when each is feeling that we have let the other down. The depth of our understandings—and misunderstandings—led to our final reckoning on the day before his death when he asked something of me.

Once when I had come for dinner, I watched Archie in a courtly manner holding a chair out for Phyllis to sit at the table, which I had rarely seen him do. He had hurt her in some way (as I knew) and he was making up. I felt that on many occasions when he held the chair for me, too.

Archie could hurt you, but he could also help you. And he had been hurt in his life, and poetry helped him to heal. Phyllis said that Archie once said to her, "My failures are my successes." His biggest terror was that someone might invade his space, might trap him, and not let him get out. Perhaps I had done that, in my sometimes smothering friendship, and in my ignorance, but he had forgiven me, and I think the trust had been restored.

Archie's Cornell office door decorated after announcement he had won the National Book Award, in 1993.

ARCHIE R. AMMONS COLLECTION RARE BOOKS & MANUSCRIPT COLLECTIONS, KROCH LIBRARY, CORNELL UNIVERSITY

: : :

Certainly the time together with Phyllis and Archie was unforgettable. They treated me generously, as did their friends. Teaching at Cornell challenged me to find my place in a new environment, and I did so in the way I had observed Archie found himself at Wake Forest: I was myself—open, friendly, humorous, and taking personal interest in every student. I boosted the students' confidence, and they boosted mine. I loved my students, and I loved teaching. I took some of them to lunch at the faculty club in the university's Statler Hotel and I had parties for the faculty at my Hanshaw Road home. (I was noted for my casual ability to pull off a party on short notice.) I spent a lot of time talking to students—some had never met their advisers—and several asked me for recommendations before I left, though I had known them only for a semester. I am certain that I was not the best writing teacher they would ever have, but I was one of their best friends in an era in which human relationships between teacher and student still mattered. I hope a few of them remember me, as I remember them—even when we have forgotten names, I have the pictures I took on the day our class met outdoors.

And I got to spend time with writers I greatly admired—Robert Morgan, a native North Carolinian, and his wife Nancy, and Grace and James McConkey (whose memory book I love), who invited me to their wonderful homes in the country, and I was invited to lunch in the faculty club with Alison Lurie. Poet Phyllis Janowitz was good company, a good teacher, lively and generous, and one of the regulars at Archie's table in the Temple of Zeus. Stephanie Vaughan, chair of the writing division, and Michael Koch, editor of *Epoch* magazine, lived downtown, where they gardened, and gave a good party—she had written a terrific book of stories, *Sweet Talk*, and had studied with Wallace Stegner at Stanford. On the April day in the halls of the English Department when we heard that Stegner had died in a car accident, we all felt with Stephanie the loss of the "Dean" of Western Literature and the founder of one of the first and best MFA programs.

While at Cornell, I was working on a history of North Carolina women (it is good to put some distance on one's subject) and sought out Professor Mary Beth Norton, the great women's historian, and we had several good conversations about our work. I especially enjoyed graduate students, but I often felt as intimidated by the greatness of Cornell as Archie felt when he went to Berkeley (Phyllis said she never met a Southerner at Berkeley; I have already mentioned the other Southerner, Bob Morgan, at Cornell.) Nevertheless, I was so outspoken that I think I was not seen as a stereotypical Southern lady. I walked out of more than one meeting of women's studies when I felt excluded. Once when I felt snubbed by a Man of Importance, I snubbed him right back: Phyllis later said it was the only time I had ever disappointed her, but I was not apologetic. Perhaps I had learned something from Archie about standing my ground. Phyllis herself never wavered in her own impeccable manners. She put on a lavish reception for me at their house in Cayuga Heights, and the food was out of this world. Friends came early, ate well, and stayed late. I reminded Phyllis of the awful meal I had ordered when we celebrated Archie's Bollingen Prize at Wake Forest and she had turned it into a feast. But nothing like the spread she set in her great room, looking toward Lake Cayuga. What a day that was—and I the honored guest. I loved it, and Archie sat in his chair and watched me and beamed.

When I gave a reading at the A.D. White House, I was a nervous wreck and read badly a few new poems I had written—mostly about falling down gorges, which was my occasional nightmare. Two dear students rushed up afterward to ask why I hadn't told them I was scared of gorges—they would have walked across the bridge with me. Archie asked me to read the chapter I had published in *For the People of North Carolina* on the disappearance of the small North Carolina town of Gibson, which he called "one of the jewels of poetry," and I did. The response was good, and I slowly began to realize that my gift really was prose, especially prose about places. My next books would be in that direction, and knowing how much Archie admired my homage to a small town set me on a path I had not considered. Later, I would write books about the Southern gardens of Elizabeth Lawrence; domestic settings for North Carolina women; and Eleanor Roosevelt's private cottage at Hyde Park called Val-Kill. I think the essay on Gibson and Gibson's wonderful oldtimers, which Archie often singled out for praise, turned me toward my true subjects.

Three times a week I enjoyed going to the campus, and the book store, art museum, exercise center, and library. Someone told me that

I had been assigned the basement office in Goldwin Smith that had been Vladimir Nabokov's and his wife, Vera's—she drove him to campus, carried his briefcase and books, sat on the front row in his classes and took notes, and seemed often to grade his exams. They had come to Ithaca in 1948 with their son, Dimitri, for Nabokov's second academic appointment in the U.S. He taught at Cornell until 1959. (See Gavriel Shapiro's *Nabokov at Cornell*, which includes Dimitri's reminiscence of Ithaca, and Stacy Shiff's "The Genius and Mrs. Genius"). For Nabokov's centennial conference held at Cornell in 1998, a dedication of the Nabokov Commemorative Plaque was held outside of Nabokov's office, 278 Goldwin Smith Hall, on the second floor. Perhaps I was using an earlier basement office before he moved up, but I rather suspect that it was a joke played on me—or perhaps the myth simply grew to be a fact among visiting artists assigned that office.

After a heavy Ithaca snow, Emily, who was living in Ithaca as a visiting writer at Cornell, walked to the Quad with Archie, where architectural students had made sofas from the snow, and Archie sat down for a portrait by Emily Herring Wilson, 1993.

: : :

My students at Cornell were diverse and open. One class was from the School of Arts and Sciences and the others were from one of the public colleges. I liked them all, and there wasn't much difference between the private (Ivy League) and the public sides (state supported). I showed Archie the stories one male student kept turning in that were mostly excremental and sexual, and Archie said that he was testing me. I wasn't shocked—but I was annoyed, and his classmates told him to cut it out. Charlotte "Chippy" Fogle, the widow of a famous English professor, Ed Fogle, took me to a dance recital and warned me that the dancers would be naked. They looked pretty much as I had expected. In one class, a favorite of mine was a shy boy from a nearby small town, and I would love to know where he is now. He wrote experimental fiction, influenced by one of his favorite writers, which I knew nothing about, and I didn't have the slightest idea how to help him, but I thought that what he really needed was a mother and not a teacher, so I lapsed into my nurturing role with him. At a school as big as Cornell, so many get lost; they really do. But I had explored the area and seen that it wasn't very different from the South—it was pure Appalachian just a few miles out of town.

When I wondered over to the Ag side of the campus from Goldwin Smith Hall on the Quad, I followed signs to the Department of Pomology and looked into an open office door and saw a professor taking a nap with his feet on the desk. I loved the casualness of it all. He woke up to my question: did he know anything about the York Imperial apple, said in my family to have been propagated by a Quaker relative in Pennsylvania? Without taking his feet off his desk, he reached behind him and took down an encyclopedia of pomology and then, he found the name of Jonathan Jessop, one of my early nineteenth century ancestors. It amazed me that I had found anyone in his office and more amazing that he put his hands right on the history of my relative, Jonathan Jessop. Imagine, finding Jessops in Ithaca, New York! I had grown up in my great-grandfather's house in Columbus, Georgia, where the named J E S S O P had been poured into the concrete sidewalk. I passed Jessop Road every day as I entered the Cornell campus. The region had had a group of Quaker settlers, from which my ancestors must have descended in their movement into North Carolina and Georgia.

I liked the mix of disciplines at Cornell—the vet school, the fruit orchards, the labor union seminars—and I enjoyed going with Archie to Plantation Gardens and having him point out to me a flock of red-winged blackbirds. And I enjoyed going to the Ornithology Lab on Hanshaw Road—I'm still a member of the Cornell Laboratory of Ornithology— and I have learned some bird songs. The farmers market on Saturday mornings, Wegman's Grocery, the state parks—Phyllis's favorites became mine. She took me to Aurora to see the McKenzie-Childs collection of porcelains and to buy me a pitcher—magical! I surprised them both by skiing over for supper at their house—Archie stood at the great window and laughed as he saw me struggle up the hill. We were brother and sister, and we played together, as he had with his sisters so long ago. When the architectural students built a suite of furniture out of ice and snow on the Cornell Quad, Archie and I sat down on the sofas and posed for our picture.

In May when my daughters, Julie and Sally, flew to Ithaca to drive with me back to North Carolina, I was ready to go home to family, and I understood better Archie's need to get back to Ithaca. It had all been a sort of dream—a chance to learn a different landscape and meet strangers and bring my way of being and teaching and entertaining to new friends. But I was like Archie, who had left Berkeley without feeling that he had ever mastered it (he didn't finish the master's degree he was working on). And I felt the way he described feeling when he first came to Cornell—inadequate. But I was proud, too, that I had done well enough. And Archie was proud of me. He autographed *The Really Short Poems of A.R. Ammons* "For Emily Wilson, conqueror of our territory. From Archie Ammons, 2 March 93 Ithaca."

Farewells

Archie had had serious health issues over the years which we had discussed, but I was not prepared for his call in January 2000 telling me that he had been diagnosed with terminal cancer. We were both almost speechless. I asked him if anything helped him now and he said no.

Not even having written so often about death and dying? I asked. That doesn't make a difference?

No, not at all, he said.

"I am a sick puppy," he'd whimper as he wandered up and down the halls of the English Department saying his last goodbyes before moving to Kendal at Ithaca Retirement Community for his last year—and, for the last month, into Hospice care. Phyllis and I talked, and they both were stoic. John was stunned. He confessed that he had always been "a Mama's boy" because Phyllis had been the one to take him so many places to be entertained, but Archie was a loving father who read to him and whose poems for him have left John with a legacy unlike any other. Vida and I were devastated. Archie was quiet on the phone, but we talked often. In late February 2001, Phyllis called to tell me and Ed to come at once. I had not realized how soon that call would come.

Losing Archie was unthinkable. Vida had already flown to Ithaca to be with her beloved brother, and I was comforted by knowing that we would be with her.

Ed and I were going to see Archie for the last time, and I braced myself for the flight from North Carolina (I was as terrified of flying as he had been) and for the Northern weather that Archie for so many years had been turning into poetry. I could scarcely breathe the winter air on February 24, 2001, a cold February afternoon, treacherous with ice and shadows. The kind of day the poet A.R. Ammons had written about for some 35 winters in Ithaca

But we were not prepared to see him die.

: : :

Archie looked up from the bed and smiled and whispered, "Well, look what the cat dragged in." (Oh, death, where is thy sting?)

I laughed. And thought of his poem "Dying in a Mirthful Place," written when he still had nearly 50 years to live: *and turning to death said / I thought you knew propriety*.

His smile was thin and drawn, his head bony, his body skeletal, he was in pain. But his sardonic wit spoke from the very lip of the grave. I leaned over to make sure that I had heard him.

"Stand up," he commanded, his voice still a whisper, and I did. He looked at me for a long time with a quiet acceptance, and then he asked, with such tenderness, "How is your mother?" (My father had recently died, and when I later told my mother of Archie's concern for her, she wept.) In a few minutes of whispered, broken conversations, there was a sudden calm inhabiting the room, and then he said, "Bring John," who had come from California to be with him and had left the room when I came in.

I went out and motioned to John to come in with me, and he did.

Archie looked at us each, for a long time.

And then he said, "Now, go."

I said, "I'll see you in the spirit world."

Archie closed his eyes and smiled.

Phyllis asked Ed if he would read something from *The Book of Common Prayer*. Ed chose a poem he and I have always found very comforting, and he read:

> O Lord, support us all the day long, until the shadows lengthen and the evening comes, and the busy world is hushed, and the fever of life is over, and our work is done. Then in thy mercy grant us a safe lodging, and a holy rest, and peace at the last. *Amen*.

And we left the room.

The next morning, Ed and I and Phyllis and John went to breakfast at nearby Friendly's, a favorite of Archie's and Phyllis's. The waitress knew to keep their coffee hot. When we got back to Archie's room, Vida, who had been staying with him, said, "He's gone."

Archie clearly had been both mystified and terrified. But by the time he was close to drawing his last breath, he had become what his wife Phyllis described as "the most stoic person I ever knew." He waited to be turned, never complaining of the pain. When Vida had nursed him during one of his illnesses, she had said, "He was the sweetest little boy you ever saw."

Now, all anxiety and anger gone, it seemed, he closed his eyes. And he left us. His last words were, "My God!"

It was February 25, 2001, one week after his 75th birthday. I thought of this line of his:

Nothing's going to become of anyone except death.

We had known one another across time and space. And so the thirty years of our friendship passed all too quickly, and then it was all over, save for memory.

COURTSEY OF JOHN R. AMMONS

Vida Ammons Cox and Phyllis Ammons, with Archie's framed watercolor of grapes behind them, Kendal, Ithaca, NY

Vida Ammons Cox

Under the outer arms of the Chinaberry umbrella
...we stand in our diagonal of height,
Mona singing her clear, gospel-singing, happy
    soprano,
devotional gems, songs of deliverance, glory
trains and royal telephones,
Vida, her thin-faced pale alto self-taught
coming like whippoorwills weary with sleep, next
in height, and I, shortest,
too young to more than keep the tune,
singing together, together to the sandhill fields,
to whatever moves in with night over the pines...
three singing in the deep-lying Carolina country
far from town
'prettiest thing I ever heard'
eyes lost in the green blood of night's tears
of old inherited sorrows grainy & wasted as the
    land,
beautiful, wasted as the years in
the mother's face, in the father's hands.

—*from* **"Chinaberry,"** *by* **A.R. AMMONS**

I think Archie's sister Vida Ammons Cox deserves a unique place in this memoir of Archie. Two years apart, they were playmates as children, and they loved one another so dearly for the rest of their lives. Vida and I have had many memorable times together—more than once we drove together to Ithaca, the last time to pack up Archie's watercolors, which he had given to me when he and Phyllis were moving to Kendal. We visit and talk often. Here is a little window into our friendship.

Ed and I made many trips to see Vida in Clarkton, where one of our favorite things to do is to go to Dale's Seafood Restaurant on Lake Waccamaw for an oyster roast. She lives a mile or so just out of Clarkton and is expert at negotiating the back country roads to Lake Waccamaw. We have gotten to know her son Johnny and his wife, JoAnn. When Allen, her oldest son, retired as a pilot for American Airlines, he moved from Florida back to Clarkton, to help his mother and his brother during planting and harvesting season. Sometimes they are joined by their youngest brother, Jeffrey, and each boy knows how to operate farm equipment and to study the weather; their father owned several farms and they worked there while they were growing up.

We also enjoyed sitting on Vida's back porch to watch the hummingbirds at her feeders, looking at her collection of books by her brother, and enjoying her Southern cooking. Some of Archie's watercolors hang in every room. She has had a "ladies' luncheon" for me and invited her church friends she still sees, but they are fewer in number, and recently she has lost her best ones, and the losses weigh heavily upon her. But nothing hurt her more than Archie's death, and we talk about the times we drove to Ithaca together, the morning we were there when he died. Then it is a sorrowful time, and we don't know what to say, but it is a comfort to have been with him together.

What has meant the most to me has been seeing Archie's native heath, and how much he and Vida were alike: their quick sense of humor, their fast driving, their devotion to one another, their remembrances of their childhood. And their fierce family pride. Each year hundreds of local students from middle school to high school submit original poems for the A.R. Ammons Poetry Competition, and the winners are

Ed Wilson, Vida Cox, and Emily Wilson at the cottage of Johnny and JoAnn Cox, Lake Waccamaw, 2017
photo by Jeffrey Cox

recognized at a gala evening held in the auditorium of the Southeastern Community College, and the local newspaper, *The News Reporter*, prints page after page of the winners. Some of Archie's paintings are exhibited at the college gallery, where Davidson professor Elizabeth Mills has lectured on the connections between his paintings and poems; in other programs, Alex Albright, professor of English at East Carolina University, has joined Ray Wise, a local scholar and Ammons biographer, in talking about Ammons's work. Alex conducted one of the best interviews I've read with Archie in a motel room in Greenville, N.C. just a few hours after he had read poems publicly, at ECU, for the first time since his bypass surgeries. In the interview in the *North Carolina Literary Review*, I have never heard Archie so relaxed—he jokes and laughs. He did find some time that he really could come home again when he was with people he trusted. Albright also published a charming collection of Ammons poems called *The Mule Poems* and edited Phyllis's favorite of all of Archie's books, *The North Carolina Poems*. Archie's and Phyllis's son, John, and other family members and friends made a major gift toward establishing an Ammons scholarship for students at the local community college.

Archie's most insisted upon requirement in a relationship was trust. I think he didn't trust many people, seldom trusted strangers, because he always mistrusted their motives—he thought they wanted something of him. But he always trusted his family—Vida most of all—perhaps because their love had nothing to do with his poetry. In the importance he gave to family and home, I think he was drawn back time and again to Columbus County, though he could not settle there. He was too conflicted about the history of the South and his childhood struggles on the farm, and too loyal to ever truly leave Cornell. And he was also too glad to have found a home for himself and his family in Ithaca, which Phyllis and John loved, ever to turn away from Cornell, even though he also often felt like an expatriate. "I'm a Southerner," Archie said often, in one way or another: "That feeling of home does not go away; it remains a part of you."

COURTSEY OF JOHN R. AMMONS

Archie as a teenager

Archie, about 18 years old

COURTSEY OF JOHN R. AMMONS

Two Poems by A.R. Ammons

Keeping Track

It's not going to be again the way it was:
Silver won't come up from the pasture again

and stand, head low, dozing by the gate:
the sow won't strike mouthfuls of wiregrass

all day for a rushed bed to farrow in:
I won't ever again hear my father at dusk

holler leatherbritches from the woodsroad
coming home or feel the start that things might

once be all right: the plank fence of the barnyard
is down and gone, cornerposts rotted holes:

when my memory goes, my father's never adzed
and mauled those boards from swamp-cut logs.

Between Each Song

I once would have said my sister Vida but now
I can just say my sister because the other

sister is gone: you didn't know Mona, lovely
and marvelous Mona, so you can't feel the

flooded solar plexus that grips me now: but
you may know (I don't know if I hope you will

or hope you won't—tossups between having and
holding) but you may know someone of your own

I don't quite know the pang for as you do: I
know but don't believe Mona is gone: she is

still so much with me, I can hardly tell I lost
anything when I lost so much: love is a very

strange winding about when it gets lost in
your body and especially when it can't find

the place to go to, the place it used to find: Mona is
in my heart in a way that burns my chest until

my eyes water: are you that way: even in the
midst of business I could think of caring for

you for that: but my sister Vida and I used
to have to daub (we called it dob) the baccer

barn: cracks between the uneven-log sides
had to be filled airtight with clay so the

furnace and flues could 'cure' the tobacco
with slow, then high heat: we would dig a

bucket of clay from the ditch by the road
where streaks of white and red clay ran, add

water for a thick consistency, then climb the
rafters inside the barn and dob the cracks:

An Email from Phyllis

I went for a walk over the dunes again this morning
to the sea,
then returned right along
the surf
rounded a naked headland
and returned
along the inlet shore:

—*from* ***"Corsons Inlet"*** *by* A.R. AMMONS

Phyllis and I were close friends during Archie's life, and after his death, she turned to me sometimes daily, asking my advice about various matters having to do with his estate. She came to North Carolina, I came to Ithaca. The walls of our house in Winston-Salem are filled with many favorite Ammons paintings, including two very large, somber self-portraits unlike any others; many small, playful self-portraits; and some of his early paintings in which he included words and poems. My efforts to promote his watercolors, which I think he hoped I could do, include a 2020 major exhibit at the Poetry Foundation in Chicago. In 1999 before leaving the house on Cayuga Heights Road for Kendal, he showed me all the stacks of paintings he was giving me and urged me not to let them be a "burden" to look after; he himself did not have the energy to know what to do. So I wonder: was this a reason why he "depended on me"? He showed them off with great pride, neatly stacked on closet shelves, cautioning me to keep the corners square. I was both overwhelmed by the enormity of the gift and uncertain about how to proceed. And with this memoir I turn my full attention toward being a good steward of this amazing gift and hope that in time he will be better known for his paintings.

My daughter Sally and her partner, Carolyn, use Phyllis's dining room chairs in their bungalow in Durham. Sally had gone with me to see Phyllis after Archie's death, and Phyllis had treasured Sally's presence. When Sally and her sister, Julie, were younger, and went to Ithaca and a camp nearby in a glorious state park, Phyllis and Archie had insisted on "looking after" them. When Phyllis came to Wake Forest for a seminar and exhibit of Archie's paintings, she and John had dinner with Eddie. My friendship with John continues—he works as a sound engineer in San Francisco and lives in Mill Valley, California, with his wife, Wendy, and their children, Matthew and Jasmine. Ed and I continued to see Vida: our families belong to one another.

Almost a year after Archie's death, Phyllis took what she called "a winter vacation" to visit family members on the New Jersey shore, her "home country," where she and Archie had lived with her parents in the 1950s in their grand house on the boardwalk. They had returned from Berkeley and Archie worked then for 12 years for her father in the glass business. He was also writing and sending out poems, and he began taking watercolor lessons at a local arts and crafts workshop. One of Archie's most famous poems, "Corsons Inlet," was written during this period about a place where he loved to walk and watch. This is one of the few emails Phyllis wrote to me and Ed.

NORTHFIELD NJ HISTORY MUSEUM

Phyllis, far right, with her siblings and their mother, Margaret, aboard ocean liner bound for South America, 1933

Ocean City, NJ
Mid-January [2002]

The morning was cold and brilliant. Earlier I had watched the sun rise from the green water. We were leaving that day, and although I had for several days looked out on an unusually calm ocean, I had not yet ventured out to the boardwalk much less to the beach.

I put on my heavy winter coat, walked to the outside door, down the balcony steps, and I was on the boardwalk. The air was bracing but not too cold and I walked fast for a block or so. I looked to the deserted beach, the fine sand broken by tufts of grass on gently sloping dunes and, seeing ahead a flight of stairs to the strand, walked down and headed for the water's edge, my shoes still on and not sinking into the morning-damp sand. It was a wide strand and as I walked I could see that the tide was starting to come in. Soon I reached the ocean, heard the soothing lapping of the waves breaking on the shore, stood there feeling engulfed by the rhythm and vastness of the water, and all the time thinking of Archie, how much he loved the ocean. Not since he died had I felt so close to him, nor missed him more. It was a moment of profound sadness and renewal. Finally, scrambling against the coming tide, I turned and walked back to the boardwalk and the hotel.

Love to you and Ed
Phyllis

Archie in New Jersey, 1955

COURTSEY OF JOHN R. AMMONS

Afterword

In my Prologue I began with Archie's statement to me in one of our last conversations, "I depend on you," but that was only part of Archie's instructions for me in one of our weekly phone conversations in the last year of his life, when, ill with terminal cancer, he knew that his time was running out. Phyllis had almost single-handedly moved them out of the house on Cayuga Heights Road into a cottage in the nearby retirement community of Kendal. He hated moving but knew it was for the best and was ready for Phyllis now to make all the decisions he alone used to make. Although there were many retired Cornell families at Kendal, Archie was lonely, and he called me often, perhaps called others. He missed his trips to his office in Goldwin Smith Hall and his conversations with colleagues, and he missed views from his living room of sunsets over Lake Cayuga. Phyllis had to continue clearing out the house and running errands to get the supplies they needed. It was an exhausting task, but Archie knew that she was capable of doing anything that needed doing.

From the phone call in which he said "I depend on you," I wrote a few other phrases from that conversation on that slip of paper. They are:

"Take a look at *Glare*. It is thin, but I took risks. I particularized. But now and then the story's there."

He added, enigmatically, "I do have something I'd call an autobiography, a journal in prose about what happened as time went by, starting in 1947. It is book-length. I have it in a single box."

What did this mean for me to do?

Most of Archie's papers have been cataloged in Special Collections at the Cornell Library, and researchers have found no "single box," either at Cornell or in the smaller collection at East Carolina University. As biographer and Cornell professor Roger Gilbert completes his long anticipated two-volume biography of Archie, perhaps he will make more sense of this remark since he has worked in the collection so meticulously.

It is as mysterious to me as anything. Here's what I've tried to do: take him at his word, that he was giving me some kind of direction forward, how he wanted to be remembered, but I have no certainty at all. Perhaps someday I will have more.

I began by reading as many of the journals and letters as I could. Kevin McGuirk edited an excellent selection, An Image for Longing, which is useful for anyone wanting easy access to some of the best of the Ammons papers—letters and journals, especially—at Cornell. But what I have written is no scholarly biography, and I limit myself now, as I conclude, to a tiny fraction of what's in those papers.

In 1949, while still a student at Wake Forest, Archie wrote in a journal about the role of the poet, and he sent this description in a letter to Phyllis that starts to lay out his life's ambition to be a poet:

> Poetry needs a Messiah; it needs some irrepressible, high-larking, unmolded gentleman to step in and scatter the high-browed dictators of poetry in the manner Jesus scattered the traders...Poet, if you want to be vulgar, be vulgar; if you want to deny God, do so; if you want to soar, soar.

Archie could be bawdy ("vulgar," he called it). He warns Phyllis in courtship letters in which he begs her to marry him that she must not expect him to be perfect. In *Glare* he apologizes for those he has hurt. He declares how much he has loved us all. I am not going to be the critic trying to interpret meaning. Others will be quick (or slow) to do that. I will go on pondering what his last telephone call was saying to me.

But for now, I want Archie to have the last word, from *Glare*, the poem he told me to "take a look at" in our last conversation:

COURTSEY OF JOHN R. AMMONS

Archie playing piano in the Hanshaw Road home, which he and Phyllis purchased in October 1966.

. . . I long for a poem

so high, but not too high, where every agony
can be acknowledged as a quiver in the easy

ongoing of the pacific line: love is a kind of
violence; death takes hold sometimes violently:

grief's gusts nearly break your ribs; we deal as
best we can with these but running through and

rising, is the constant will, that longs for
companionship with an all-keeping indifference

. . . I try to
hide the old fool playing the fool, but you

hear, don't you, the young man, still young,
still under there saying yes yes to the new

days darkened howsomever: it is a sad song but
it sings and wants to sing on and on and when

it can no more it wants someone else to sing:
To sing is everything . . . .

The End

An A.R. Ammons Timeline

Introduced by **ALEX ALBRIGHT**

WHEN I GO BACK TO MY HOME COUNTRY

A.R. Ammons's home country—"the deep lying Carolina country"—was in flat and swampy Columbus County on the Carolinas' border, a county away from the ocean. In 1930s rural North Carolina, living without electricity or indoor plumbing on a subsistence farm on a dirt road was more a fact of life than a marker of poverty, as has been too often said of the upbringing that Archie shared with sisters Vida and Mona. With family, food, a paid-for farm with crops and friends to help plant and harvest those crops, necessary animals, and a community church, they didn't think of themselves as poor. "They make it sound awful," Vida sometimes complained. The farm, she said, was their father's "old homestead where *his* brothers and sisters grew up."

Their twelve uncles and aunts: John O'Neil, Mary Ellen, James, Laura, Lizzie Magnolia, Franklin, Sarah (or Aunt Mitt), Ellen, Addie Victoria, Rachel Hettie, Kate Missouri, Lottie Lee, and their dad, William.

Of Archie's generation, there were six born to William M. and Della McKee Ammons:

Mona, born October 21, 1920.

Vida Lee, born March 14, 1924.

Randolph, who became the poet known as A.R., born Feb. 18, 1926.

Of two younger brothers, one died on his birth day, June 4, 1931, and the other, Willie Ebert, died on May 16, 1930, not yet two years old. A sister born December 20, 1922 died on March 4, 1923.

Mona, Vida and Archie grew up as farm kids. Vida recalled, in the 2004 essay in which she listed her aunts and uncles, that planting and harvesting were often done "with cousins our age who worked with us and it was fun to be with them."

Otherwise, not a lot to do: "Entertainment, travel, and educational opportunities were very limited in our community during the Depression years," Vida wrote. "Archie and I spent a lot of time playing in the wooded area on the farm, fishing in the pond, improvising our own toys, swings, and tree houses."

When I asked Archie in a 1992 interview what amusement was around the farm, he echoed his sister: "I had to invent it basically and I did it mostly, and that's how I became, I think, attached to ponds and mudbanks and ditchbanks, brierberries, things of that kind."

That natural landscape of Columbus County informs much of his poetry, and his immersion into it as a child set him on a lifetime of exploring systems, patterns, and aberrations.

But in addition to that natural landscape, the homeplace and his family, Archie also includes in his poetry shout-outs to the home country places he knew in his time: Vinland, Chadbourn, Hallsboro, Green Swamp, Nakina, Lumber River, Fair Bluff, Spring Branch Church, Gause's Landing, Whiteville and South Whiteville, Mays Landing, Soul's Swamp, New Brunswick, Shalotte, Lake Waccamaw, and Green Sea, just over the state line in South Carolina.

Archie was named simply "Randolph Ammons" at birth. There was no Archie, officially, until he was grown. His father, in registering his son's name at the Columbus County Courthouse in Whiteville, perhaps registered also a personal statement about his in-laws when he omitted the intended "Archibald," which was his wife's father's name. "I discovered many years later there was no Archie Randolph Ammons," he told me. "My father had simply left his wife's father out of the picture. I had been all that time, however, called Archie, not with a 'b-a-l-d.' So I wanted to keep that name. So I paid $1.80 or whatever it was to have the name changed to Archie Randolph Ammons."

That change didn't happen until 1967, when he was preparing passport information for a fellowship to Rome, a detail that comes from Ken McGuirk's excellent book, *An Image for Longing: Selected Letters and Journals of A.R. Ammons, 1951–974*. McGuirk has assembled a lively and revealing collection of Archie's letters sent and unsent along with journal entries, such as the ambitious one included in this book, from 1951, and which we have titled "Ten Years Ago I Was" after its opening line.

This timeline is decidedly place and family-centric and as a result denotes some events that might not have made it into a more traditionally constructed timeline. The dates that indicate Archie's driving trips home and his inquiries for work at the Columbus County *News* and the University of North Carolina are among several other incidents revealed in the work collected by McGuirk, whose book leaves off about the time Emily's begins, in 1974, when she and her husband, Ed, became friends with Archie and Phyllis Ammons during the sabbatical year Archie spent in Winston-Salem.

The driving home details—he drove on all his visits home—in this timeline are made more intense because of how Emily has so powerfully narrated several of her "driving with Archie" stories.

1943 Archie graduates from Whiteville High School.

1944–46 In U.S. Navy, stationed at Camp Peary, Williamson, VA; Key West, FL; and aboard the battleship escort USS *Gunason*.

Summer 1946 Enters Wake Forest College.

Spring 1947 Meets and begins courting his Spanish teacher, Phyllis Plumbo.

1949 Graduates from Wake Forest College.

Sep 1949 Begins work as school principal and teacher at Hatteras Elementary School.

Nov 26, 1949 Marries Phyllis Plumbo in Atlantic City, NJ, and they return to Hatteras.

1950 Leaves Hatteras at conclusion of school year; enrolls in undergraduate courses in English at UC-Berkeley, with plans to work towards a Master's. Meets Josephine Miles, poet and English professor at Berkeley.

Mar 22, 1950 Mother, Lucy Della McKee Ammons, dies at 62.

Jun 7, 1951 Takes last exam of semester at UC-Berkeley, begins packing for return to Northfield, NJ, where he begins work for Phyllis's father's glass company, Friedrich & Dimmock.

Feb 1952 Resumes course work at UC-Berkeley.

Jun 1952 After learning of his father's illness, leaves Berkeley; visits family in NC; then to NJ, living first in Phyllis's family home and then nearby in Northfield.

Mar 1953 First poems accepted by the *Hudson Review*.

The Plumbo home in Northfield, NJ

1955 Self-publishes first book, *Ommateum*, with W.H. Dorrance, for $480.

Dec 9–11, 1955 Drives from NJ to visit with family in NC for weekend; offers to write a regular column, "Thoughts," for *Columbus County News*.

1956 Wake Forest College closes in Wake Forest, NC, and opens in Winston-Salem.

Apr 16, 1959 Inquires about possibility of teaching creative writing at UNC-CH.

Aug 1960 Helps establish *Country Club Woman* magazine as its literary editor.

Apr 4, 1961 Writes "Nelly Myers."

Aug 1961 Receives fellowship at Breadloaf Writers Conference.

Sep 1961 Drives to Charlotte to visit sister Mona.

May 19, 1962 Writes sister Vida from Northfield, NJ, reporting that *Country Club Woman* has folded, and that "I've been thinking of coming to Caylina for a spell" and will "maybe take the job" Vida's husband has offered him.

Sep 1962 Visits family in Columbus County, his father having had his leg amputated.

Sep 16, 1962 Asks UNC-CH again about a teaching position "for a year or so."

1964 Joins English faculty at Cornell.

Jan 29, 1966 Son John born in Ithaca.

Apr 12, 1966 John adopted by Archie and Phyllis, who subsequently celebrate this date annually as "Family Day."

Oct 1966 Family moves to 606 Hanshaw Road, Ithaca.

Archie in Mallorca, 1967
photo by Phyllis Ammons

1966 Father, William "Will" Ammons, dies at 71.

1967 Receives Guggenheim Fellowship; with Phyllis and John, goes to Rome. Decides to return early and the Ammons family spends the first months of 1968 living in Ocean City, NJ before returning to Ithaca.

Sep 27, 1969 Writes to sister "Vida and all": "I haven't stayed away from North Carolina this long since I was born."

Spring 1970 Drives to Columbus County for five days while Phyllis and John stay in NJ for their vacation.

May 29, 1972 Awarded honorary doctoral degree from Wake Forest University.

1974 Cornell establishes Goldwin Smith Chair, an endowed professorship that Archie will hold for the rest of his career. John, who was 6 at the time, recalls wondering, "Why didn't he already have a chair? Where did he sit?"

1974–75 On sabbatical leave from Cornell, teaches at Wake Forest, where he, Phyllis and John live in the faculty neighborhood and John enrolls in school.

Summer 1974 With Emily Wilson, Betty Leighton, and Isabel Zuber, establishes Jackpine Press in Winston-Salem.

Dec 1, 1974 Writes the poems "For Emily Wilson" and "For Edwin Wilson."

1975 Wins Bollingen Prize for *Sphere*, an occasion celebrated at Wake Forest University with a program in Dec. 1974 featuring remarks by Harold Bloom and Josephine Jacobsen.

Summer 1975 Leaves Winston-Salem and stays with Phyllis's family in Ocean City, NJ, where he writes "Summer Place."

Dec 1976 Begins painting watercolors at home on Hanshaw Road, Ithaca.

Apr 1977 With Phyllis goes to Winston-Salem to read at Reynolda House.

May 7, 1977 With Phyllis, Vida, Emily and Ed Wilson drives to Wake Forest, NC, to see the original Wake Forest College campus.

Summer 1977 Archie, Phyllis, and John drive to Ocean Isle, NC to vacation with Archie's sisters and families.

Jun 1980 Teaches summer writing workshop in Critz, VA.

1981 Awarded MacArthur Fellowship

Jun 1–13, 1981 Teaches poetry workshop at Reynolda House Museum of American Art, Winston-Salem, NC.

1983 Exhibits watercolors at Morehead Planetarium on campus of UNC-CH.

May 10, 1986 With Phyllis, participates in "The Home Country of A.R. Ammons" symposium presented by the North Carolina Humanities Council at Salem College, Winston-Salem, with Helen Vendler keynote speaker.

1986 Receives the North Carolina Award in Literature at Raleigh.

Jul 1988 Son John leaves Ithaca for West Coast, follows the Grateful Dead for a while, and enrolls at San Francisco State University.

1989 Suffers heart attack, hospitalized in Ithaca.

1990 Has triple bypass surgery.

Dec 1991–Jan 1992 With Phyllis, visits sister Vida in Clarkton and stays in Wilsons' cottage in Swansboro, NC.

Jan 14, 1992 Presents public reading at East Carolina University and subsequently agrees to be Staff Poet for the *North Carolina Literary Review.*

1992 Moves from Hanshaw Road to 423 Cayuga Heights Road, Ithaca; Ammons collection established at Cornell.

Jan 16, 1993 Emily Wilson drives to Ithaca for semester as visiting writer at Cornell.

May 3, 1993 Receives honorary doctorate from East Carolina University.

May 6, 1993 Emily's last class at Cornell; she drives home to Winston-Salem with daughters Sally and Julie Wilson.

1994 *North Carolina Poems* published by NC Wesleyan College Press as a *North Carolina Literary Review* book.

Mar 1994 Drives to Hillsborough, NC for visit with sister Mona, who is in a nursing home.

Apr 7–9 1995 "Say Things and Gather About," a symposium with Archie and Cornell colleagues Ken McClane and Alice Fulton, held at Wake Forest University. One seminar session was led by Wake Forest President Tom Hearn, who loved Archie's poems and with his wife, Laura, had become good friends with the Ammonses.

May 1994 Visits sister Mona in Hillsborough.

Jun 1995 Phyllis attends John's graduation from San Francisco State University, too far away for Archie to drive.

Dec 11, 1995 Sister Mona Ammons Smith dies; Archie, who is staying in Winston-Salem, drives Ed and Emily Wilson to Concord, NC for her funeral.

Feb 23, 1996 Grandson Matthew Ammons born in Mill Valley, California.

Sep 21, 1996 John Ammons and Wendy Moskow married on Stinson Beach in Marin County. "No way was Archie going to travel that far!" John recalled.

Spring 1997 With Phyllis, in residence at Wake Forest University.

May 10, 1997 Presents public reading and commencement address at UNC-Pembroke and receives honorary degree.

1998 Suffers subdural hematoma; retires fromt Cornell University.

Apr 3-4, 1998 Ammonsfest celebration at Cornell.

Jul 3, 1998 Granddaughter Jasmine Ammons born in Mill Valley, California.

1999 With Phyllis, moves to Kendal, a retirement community in Ithaca.

2000 Inducted into North Carolina Literary Hall of Fame at Weymouth, in Southern Pines; Vida accepts the award for her brother, who is too ill to travel.

Jan 20, 2001 Tells Emily in phone conversation that he is dying of cancer and that "I depend on you."

Feb 2001 Emily and Ed Wilson, John Ammons, and Vida Ammons Cox join Phyllis at Archie's bedside, where he dies on the morning of Feb. 25.

Apr 19, 2001 Memorial service at Davis Chapel, Wake Forest University.

Apr 29, 2001 Memorial service at Cornell.

Oct 11–Nov 13, 2002 "A.R. Ammons: Pattern and Possibility," a show of Ammons watercolors at Wake Forest, curated by Alex Hitchcock and Elizabeth Mills.

Mar 24, 2004 Inducted into Wake Forest University's Literary Hall of Fame.

Jun 2006 Emily Wilson and daughter Sally visit Phyllis Ammons at Kendal.

Feb 19, 2007 Emily Wilson and Jane Kelly drive to Hatteras to meet some of Archie's former students and see the village where he lived.

Oct 18, 2008–Jun 30, 2009 "A.R. Ammons's Poetry and Art: A Documentary Exhibit" presented at East Carolina University.

Jun 29, 2009 Robert M. West presents closing lecture, "The Shape/Things Will Take: Looking Ahead to the Complete Poems of A.R. Ammons," for ECU exhibit.

2010 Expanded edition of *North Carolina Poems* published by Broadstone; *Mule Poems* published by R.A. Fountain.

Nov 14–16, 2010 "Single threads unbraided," a celebration of the work of A.R. Ammons, presented at Wake Forest University, featuring "Here to Become Forever," a play adapted by Michael Huie from correspondence between Archie and Phyllis, 1947–50.

Jul 2, 2013 Phyllis Plumbo Ammons dies at 89.

2015 Southeastern Community College, Whiteville, NC, awards the first A.R. Ammons scholarship, endowed by John Ammons and friends.

Matthew and Jasmine Ammons, with their father, John R. Ammons at Taughannock Falls, NY, 2018
photo by Dawn Cramton

Dec 7, 2018 "About Ammons," a celebration at Wake Forest University of the recently published two-volume *The Complete Poems of A.R. Ammons*, with keynote address by Robert M. West, the *Complete Poems* editor.

Apr 4, 2019 Vida Lee Ammons Cox dies, not far from the Columbus County farm on which she, Archie, and Mona grew up.

Dearest Folks,

S ept. 23, 1945

T his is hardly the type of paper to write letters on, but right now it is all I have. Witsberger, that is the man who gives me my Spanish lessons' has gone ashore on liberty, so I decided to write you.

T hat doesn't work very well so I'll double space the darn thing. Vida, I just got a letter from you that says that now you are home. I'm glad you have finally finished and can relax at least, for a little while. But your letter didn't sound like you were having such a good time at home. C ertainly you must miss the girls quite a bit, but perhaps you will get over that soon.

I told Daddy that he was trying to cut too big a caper by getting on the police force, but you just can't tell him those things until he finds it out for himself. Now I hope he'll settle down for a quiet winter's rest which he needs very badly. A nyway by this time I hope he is completely well and has had no other trouble.

Relatives are just about as dull seeming to me as they are to you. To sum it all up they're just a bit to nosey, if you know what I mean. And as for wanting to see you or loving you in the slightest, they don't give a damn if they never see you again. Am I right? N o, my dear, you aren't growing old. Those hot headed little gals that used to go to school with you just couldn't control their emotions, so look at'em, a couple of dirty behined young'uns on each arm. I'm glad you aren't married yet, because a girl doesn't even know what she wants when she's only seventeen or eighteen. That is if they are anyways like a boy.

News? I've written so many letters home now that it almost embarrasses me to ask how you are. A nd besides, I've told everything I've even dreamed in the last six months. I'm well. We're in Manila. That is all.

As for Robert, I don't like him any more. If there has ever been a stuck up guy, It's Him. He thought he knew everything in the world when I came aboard, naturally I changed his mind. Then in order to get even with me for

Archie R. Ammons
Co-935
unit A-9
Camp Peary, Va.

Free

Miss Vida Lee Ammons
219 Boulevard
High Point, N.C.

Jackpine Press

Jackpine Press was founded during the summer of 1975 in Winston-Salem, by Emily Herring Wilson, Betty Leighton, and Isabel Zuber, with A.R. Ammons its first general editor. After his sabbatical year, 1974–75, at Wake Forest University, Ammons returned to Cornell University and took a less active role in Jackpine Press. In 1979–80 Wilson and Zuber sold the press to Betty Leighton, who subsequently published two volumes of stories by Josephine Jacobsen. Leighton was also the primary book reviewer for the Winston-Salem *Journal*. Jackpine went out of business in the late 1980s.

Books published by Jackpine Press, Winston-Salem

Balancing on Stones
poems by Emily Herring Wilson (1975)
Out in the Country, Back Home
poems by Jeff Daniel Marion (1976)
Orion, a poem
by Jerald Bullis (1976)
Sidetracks
poems by Clint McCown (1977)
A Walk with Raschid and Other Stories
by Josephine Jacobsen (1978)
Thirtieth Year to Heaven: New American Poets (1980)
Adios, Mr. Moxley: Thirteen Stories
by Josephine Jacobsen (1986)

Sources

Ammons, A.R. *The Complete Poems*, Robert West, ed. New York, Cornell UP, 2017: "The Arc inside and Out" (1: 642–44); "Dying is a Mirthful Place" (1: 12;) "Easter Morning" (2: 14–18); "Nelly Myers" (1: 42–45); "Summer Place" (2: 423–63); *Tape for the Turn of the Year* (1: 141–347).

---. *Changing Things*. Winston-Salem, Palemon P, 1981.

---. "I Was Born in." Typed scroll. n.d. A.R. Ammons Collection. Archives & Special Collections, Joyner Library, East Carolina U., Greenville, NC.

---. Journal entries. Archie Ammons Papers, 1945-2001. Div. of Rare and Manuscript Collections, Koch Library, Cornell University. in McGuirk: 19 May 1951 (8–9); 19 Apr. 1951 (14–5).

---. Letters to author 6 Feb. 1973, Undated [July 1975], 30 Jan. 1992, and Letter to Edwin Wilson 28 May 1983, Ammons Papers, Ammons-Wilson Correspondence, Special Collections and Archives, Z. Smith Reynolds Library, Wake Forest University; Letters to Alex Albright 9 Dec. 1991, 9 Feb. 1993, private collection of recipient; Letters to Ken Frazelle 14 Feb. 1985, in Gilbert (554), 11 Mar. 1980, private collection of recipient; Letters to Phyllis Plumbo 4 Mar. 1949, 1 May 1949. Archie Ammons Papers, 1945–2001. Div. of Rare and Manuscript Collections, Kroch Library, Cornell University.

Ammons, John R. Interviews with author, 15–16 Nov. 2010. Winston-Salem.

---. Email to author. 25 Jan. 2019.

Ammons, Phyllis Plumbo. Email to author. 21 Jan. 2002.

Bloom, Harold. "The Breaking of the Vessels." *Salmagundi* 31/32. Fall 1975–Winter 1976: 185–203.

Cox, Vida Ammons. "On 'Surprising Elements'" in Gilbert 365–66.

Crawford, Franklin. "A.R. Ammons, Twice a National Book Award Winner, Dead at 75," *Cornell Chronicle*. 26 Feb. 2001. news.Cornell.edu: 21 July 2019.

Eliot, T.S. "Little Gidding." *Four Quartets*. New York, Harcourt, 1942.

Gilbert, Roger, ed. "This Is Just a Place: An Issue Dedicated to the Life and Work of A.R. Ammons." *Epoch* 52.3 [2004].

Lehman, David. Introduction. *A.R. Ammons: Selected Poems*. American Poets Project book 20. New York: Library of America, 2006.

McClane, Ken. Email to author, 1 Jan. 2019.

McGuirk, Kevin, ed. *An Image for Longing: Selected Letters and Journals of A.R. Ammons, 1951–1974*. Victoria, British Columbia: Else Editions, 2013.

Moore, Marianne. "England." *Complete Poems of Marianne Moore*. New York: Viking, 1967.

Morgan, Robert. qtd. in Crawford.

Nabokov, Dimitri. "On Returning to Ithaca" in Shapiro 277–84.

Plumbo, Phyllis. Letters to A.R. Ammons, 15 Nov. 1949; undated [Nov. 1949]. A.R. Ammons Collection, Southern Historical Collection, Wilson Library, UNC-CH.

Schiff, Stacy. "The Genius and Mrs. Genius." *New Yorker*. 10 Feb. 1997.

Shapiro, Gavriel, ed. *Nabokov at Cornell*. Ithaca, NY: Cornell UP, 2003.

Stephenson, Shelby. Email to author, 2 May 2008.

---. Editor, *Pembroke Magazine, Ammons Issue*. 1988.

Vendler, Helen. "A.R. Ammons and Home: Dwelling in the Flow of Shapes." Lecture, NC Humanities Council seminar. Salem College, Winston-Salem. 10 May 1986. Pub. in *Southwestern Review* 72.2 Spring 1987: 150–187.

West, Robert, ed. *The Complete Poems of A.R. Ammons*. 2 vols. New York: Norton, 2017.

New Hope cemetery
photo by Diane Vitale, 2019

Index

Adams, Barry, 18

Albright, Alex, 13, 19, 142

Ambrose, Steven, 104

American Academy of Arts and Letters, 89

Ammons, A.R., anger 45, 85, 87, 94, 114-16; on poetry 67, 85, 88, 139; awards & honors: Bollingen Prize 52, 58, 88, 119, 146; American Academy of Arts and Letters, elected to 89, Guggenheim Fellowship 37, 89, 145; honorary degrees: East Carolina 146, Pembroke 103, Wake Forest 15, 145; National Book Award 88, *117*, National Book Critics Circle Award 88, NC Award in Literature, 146; NC Literary Hall of Fame, inducted into, 89, 147, Robert Frost Medal 88, Ruth Lilly Prize 88, Wake Forest Literary Hall of fame, inducted into, 148; birth, 142; books: *Bosh and Flapdoodle* 88, *Briefings* 36, *Brink Road* 84, 88; *A Coast of Trees* 88; *Changing Things* 6; *Collected Poems* 36, 54; *The Complete Poems* 6, 13, 88, 148; *Corsons Inlet* 36, 84; *Diversifications* 88; *Garbage* 88; *Glare* 88, 130, 139, 141; *Highgate Road* 88; *Lake Effect Country* 88, 96; *The Mule Poems* 6, 88, 129,148; *Tape for the Turn of the Year* 6, 36, 54-55, 57; *The North Carolina Poems* 88, 129, 148; *Northfield Poems* 36; *Ommateum* 89, 144; *The Really Short Poems* 88, 122; *Selected Poems* 88; *Selected Longer Poems 1951-1977*, 88; *The Snow Poems* 38, 88, 90; *Sphere: The Form of a Motion* 52, 54, 114, 146; *Sumerian Vistas* 88; *Tape for the Turn of the Year* 6, 36, 54-55, 57; *Uplands* 36; *Worldly Hopes* 88; fears 67, 84, 85, 110; coffee 40, 47, 53, 124, death of 2, 72, 116, 123-25, 147; family, list of aunts and uncles, 142; health, 12, 123, 125, 146, 147; homes, Royall Dr. (Winston-Salem) 38, 84; (NJ) Ocean City 24; (NY) Ithaca, Cayuga Hts. 24, *102*, 113, 119, 134, 138, Hanshaw Rd. 24, *82*, 85, 94, 96, 113, 118, *140*, 145, 146; Kendal 123, 127, 134, 138, 147; insecurities, 24, 36, 45, 86, 103, 107, 111; Navy, U.S, service in, 19, 66, 144; painting, 85-86, 87, 92, 134, 146; poems: "The Arc Inside and Out" 54; "Between Each Song" 6, 9, 32-33; "Chinaberry" 6, 126; "Chiseled Clouds" 6, 8, 76; "Corsons Inlet" 6, 134, 135; "Dying in a Mirthful Place" 124, "Easter Morning" 6, 10, 72-73, 98; "Father" 6, 8, 76; "For Edwin Wilson" 6, 8, 48, 145; "For Emily Wilson" 6, 8, 48, 50-51, 145; "For Emily Wilson, from a Newcomer" 6, 43; "Hardweed Path Going" 105; "Improvisation for the Other Way Around" 98; "I Was Born in" 6, 8, 71; "I Went Back" 6, 8, 76, 106; "Keeping Track" 6, 9, 131; "Motioning" 8, 78; "My Father, I Hollow for You" 6, 8, 78; "Nelly Myers" 6, 16, 105, 144; "Silver" 6, 105; "Still" 6, 24 , 26-27; "Small Song" 109 "Summer Place" 84-85, 146; "Ten Years ago I Was" 6, 8, 35; sabbatical, 8, 9, 21, 36, 38, 52, 84-85, 87, 88-89, 143, 151; teeth, 53, 92-93

Ammons, John R., 6, 11, 12, 13, 15, 18, *20*, *32*, 37, 38-39, 45, *47*, 68, *69*, 84-85,92, 123-24, 129, 145, 146, 147; and family, Wendy Moskow (wife) 135; (children) Matthew and Jasmine 135, 147

Ammons, Lucy Della McKee, 72, 126, 142; death, 144
Ammons, Phyllis Plumbo, 9, 11, 12, 13, 15, 18, 24, 28, 30-31, 37, 39, 46-47, *62*, 64, 67, 81, 84-85, 88, 92, 94, 96, 98, 110, 113, 114-15, 118-19, 122, 123, *125*, 129, 134, 135, *135*, 138-39, 143, 145, 146, 147, 148; cooking prowess, 19, 22, 38, 40, 45, 52, 55, 63, 88, 119, 149; dancing with Archie, *33*; marriage to Archie, 28, 30-31, 36, 144; as Spanish teacher 19, 22, *32*, 66; death, 149
Ammons, Willie Ebert, 72, 142
Ammons, William M., 35, 36, 72, 74, 77, 78, 79, 126, 131, 142, 143; death, 145
Angelou, Maya, *91*
Antiques Roadshow, 88
A.R. Ammons Lounge (Wake Forest U), 40
A.R. Ammons Poetry Competition, 75, 127
A.R. Ammons Scholarship, 129, 148
Ashbery, John, 52
Auden, W.H., 52

Baldwin, Ruth M., 81
Barkley, Alice, 98
Bloom, Harold, 13, 18, 36, *41*, 52-55
Book of Common Prayer, 124
Bragg, Nick 58, 92
Bree, Germaine, 60
Breadloaf Writers Conference, 145
Bullis, Jerald, 59, 98, 151
Byer, Kay Stripling, 92

California towns: Berkeley, 18, 19, 24, 35, 36, 66, 68, 84, 108, 118, 122, 135; Los Angeles, 108; Mill Valley, 135, 147; San Francisco, 135
Carroll, Peggy and Wally, 44
Cemeteries: New Hope Baptist Church [Columbus Co., NC] 72, 76; Pleasant Grove [Ithaca, NY]
Chappell, Fred, 59
Churches, NC: Clarkton Presbyterian, 23; New Hope Baptist, 72, 88; Spring Branch Fire Baptized Pentecostal, 54, 104, 143
Colleges: Douglass 66, Salem, 48, 89, 98, 146; Southeastern Community, 75, 129, 148; Wake Forest, 8, 13, 28, 64, *65*, 66-68, 139, 144
Coleman, Elliot, 55
Columbus, GA, 22, 121

Cook, Nancy 8
Cornell Laboratory of Ornithology, 122
Country Club Woman [magazine], 145
Cox, Sr., Allen, 23, 68, 145
Cox, Jr., Allen, 68, 127
Cox, Jeffrey, 68, 127, 128
Cox, Johnny, 68, and JoAnn, 75, 127
Cox, Vida Ammons, 9, 13, 15, 23, 37, 64, 68, 72, 75, 90, 98, 102, 103, 104, 123-125, *125*, 126-29, *128*, 132-33, 135, 142, 145, 146, 147; death, 148

Dickerman, Marion 8
Dickinson, Emily, 11, 16
Dodding, Jim, 40

Easley, Allen, 67
Eliot, T.S., 11, 59

Faulkner, William, 104
Fogle, Charlotte and Ed, 121
Ford, President Gerald and Mike, 17
Fosso, Doyle, 58
Frazelle, Kenneth, 13, 100, 106, 108-09, *109*
Friedrich & Dimmock (glass manufacturer) 36, 135, 167-68, 144
Frost, Robert, 52, 59
Fulton, Alice, 147

Gibson, Grace, 104
Gilbert, Roger, 114, 138
Gossett, Tom and Louise, 40
Green, Paul, 108

Hardy Boys, 84
Hearn, Tom and Laura, 147
Hitchcock, Alex, 147
Hopkins, Gerard Manley, 59
Huie, Michael, 149
Hymns, "How Great Thou Art," 103; "The Royal Telephone," 103; "One Step More," 104

Ingram, Maria, 58

Jacobsen, Josephine, *41*, 52-55, *56*, 59-60, 151
Jacobsen, Eric, 53, 59
Janowitz, Phyllis, 118
Jarrell, Randall, 11, 25, *25*, 59
Jessop, Jonathan, 121
Juilliard School of the Arts, 108

Kelly, Jane, 28, 45, 60, 148
Kelly, Pat, 45
Key West, FL, 144
Koch Michael, 118
Kroch, Cornell U, 138

Lakes: (NY) Cayuga, 24, 113, 119, 138; Finger, 89; (NC) Bladen, 75; Waccamaw, 74-75, 127, 143; White, 75, 127
Lawrence, Elizabeth, 8, 119
LeCarre, John, *48*
Leighton, Betty, 159-60, 145, 151
Libraries, Joyner, East Carolina U, 159-60; Z. Smith Reynolds, Wake Forest U, 40
Literary journals, *American Poetry Review*, 6; *Chelsea*, 6; *Emerson Review*, 6; *Epoch*, 6, 7, 28, 118; *Hudson Review*, 6, 15 144; *Iowa Review*, 6; *Nickelodeon*, 8, 58; *North Carolina Literary Review*, 6, 129, 146; *Pembroke Magazine*, 100; *Poetry*, 6; *the Quest*, 6
Lurie, Alison, 118

Marion, Jeff Daniel, 59, 151
Mashburn, Rick, 13, 108
McClane, Ken, 13, 100, 147, and Rochelle, 110
McCown, Clint, 54, 58-59, 151
McConkey, James and Grace, 118
MacDowell Colony, 113
McFee, Michael, 92
McGuirk, Kevin, 139, 143
Miles, Josephine, 18, 144
Mills, Elizabeth, 129, 147
Moore, Marianne, 16, 55, 59
Morehead Planetarium, 105, 146
Morgan, Robert, 55, 118,119
Mother Goose, 11
Mules: Kate, 81; Silver, 35, 81, 131; Black and Gray, 105
Murdoch, Richard, 98

Nabokov, Vladimir, Vera and Dimitri, 120
Napper Tandy (cat), 40
New Jersey towns: Atlantic City, 24, 36, 144; Ocean City, 19, 84-85, 136, 145, 146; Northfield, 32, 85, 144
New York towns: Aurora, 122; Boston, 104; Buffalo,104; Ithaca, 12, 15,17,19, 24, 68, 85, 109, 113, 115, 127, 129, 145, 146
Newspapers: Columbus County *News*, 143, 144; *The News Reporter*, *129*; Winston-*Salem Journal-Sentinel*, 44, 151
North Carolina counties: Bladen, 68; Columbus, 8, 34, 68, 70, 75, 142, 143, 144, 145, 148; Wake, 15, 64, 72, 74-75, 129, 142-43
North Carolina towns: Asheville, 74, Chadbourn, 22, 81; Chapel Hill, 105; Clarkton, 23, 75, 90, 127, 147; Concord, 147; Durham, 134; Emerald Isle, 68; Fair Bluff, 143; Gibson, 88, 119; Greenville, 129; Hallsboro, 143; Hatteras, 8, 28-29, 29, 30, 36, 144, 148; Hickory, 74; Hillsborough, 147; Marion, 74; Maxton, 104; New Bern, 74; Nakina, 143; New Hope, 105; Ocean Isle, 146; Old Salem, 40; Pembroke, 104, 105; Raleigh, 64, 66, 74, 147; Shalotte, 143; Southern Pines, 103, 105 147; Sparta, 44; Swansboro, 68, 146; Vinland 143; Wake Forest, 64, 66, 144,146; Whiteville, 23, 71, 74, 75, 105, 143, 144, 148; Wilmington, 74; Winston-Salem, 7, 11,15, 19, 28, 39, 46, 58, 60, 64, 74, 75, 81, 90, 108, 134, 143, 144, 146
North Carolina Humanities Council, 98, 146
North Carolina School of the Arts, 108
Norton, Mary Beth, 118

Phillips, Elizabeth, 15, 16
Poe, Edgar Allan, 16
Pond, Wayne, 98
Potter, Lee, 58
Publishers: Broadstone 148, Dorrance, 144; Jackpine, 7, 9, 59-60, 98, 145, 151; NC Wesleyan College, 146; Norton, 6, 7, 13, 152; R.A. Fountain, 7, 13, 149
Pulitzer Prize, 44

Restaurants: Dale's Seafood (Lake Waccamaw, NC) 75, 127; Howard Johnson's (Winston-Salem, NC) 92-93; Friendly's (Ithaca, NY) 124; Johns Hopkins Faculty Club (Baltimore, MD) 59-60; K & W Cafeteria (Winston-Salem, NC) 11, 12, 46-47; Miss Jo Williams's Cafeteria (Wake Forest, NC) 66; Shorty's (Wake Forest, NC) 64, *65*; Stephenson's Barbecue (Willow Spring, NC) 103; Village Tavern (Winston-Salem, NC) 52
R.J. Reynolds Tobacco, 38
Reynolda House and Gardens, 58, 64, 91, 92, 93, 146, 109

Reynolds, R.J. and Katherine Smith Reynolds 44, 58, 92-93, 108
Rivers, NC, Lumber, 143; White Oak, 68; Yadkin, 45, 60
Robinson Crusoe, 108
Rodtwit, Eva, 16
Rome, Italy, 37, 145
Roosevelt, Eleanor, 8, 42, 119

Schoonmaker, Don and Meyressa, 38
Shakespeare, William, 11, 58
Shapiro, Gavriel, 120
Shiff, Stacy, 120
Smith, Margaret Supple, 8
Smith, Mona Ammons, 15, 23, 37, 68, 105, 126, 132, 142, 144, 148; death, 147
South Carolina towns: Cherry Grove Beach 74; Green Sea, 143; North Myrtle Beach, 74
Southeastern Baptist Theological Seminary, 64
the South, Southerners, Southerness, 13, 18, 39, 40, 46, 67, 104, 119,127, 129
Stegner, Wallace, 118
Stephenson, Shelby, 100, 102, 103, 104-05, 107; Books, *Middle Creek Poems*, 104; Nin (Linda) 100
Stephenson, Paul, 103
Stevens, Wallace, 52
Sylvester, Gladys, 108

Temple of Zeus (Cornell U), 18, 53, 85, 94, 114, 118
Typewriters, Smith-Corona electric, 58; Underwood, 24, 48;
Tyree, Sally, 105

Universities: Cornell, 7, 9, 13, 25, 18, 21, 23, 24, 28, 36, 40, 55, 59-60, 88, 90, 94-95, 100, 113-22, 129, 145, 147, 151; racial unrest at, 110; East Carolina, 129, 138, 146, 149; Pembroke 103, 147; Rutgers, 66; San Francisco State, 146, 147; Stanford, 118; UNC-Chapel Hill, 7, 92, 143, 144, 145; UNC-Greensboro, 59; Virginia Commonwealth, 59; Virginia Tech, 92; Wake Forest, 7,12, 15, 16, 18, 21, 22, 37, 38, 40, 52, 58, 60, 84, 87-89, 96, 98, 104, 110, 113, 114, 118, 144, 147, 147, 151; UC- Berkeley, 66, 144; U of Wisconsin, 60; Yale, 13, 18, 36, 111

Vaughan, Stephanie, 118
Vendler, Helen, 13, 52, 72, 98, 146
Virginia towns: Critz, 92, 146; Williamson 144

Wake Forest Medical School, 64
Warren, Robert Penn, 95
West, Robert M., 6, 148
Whitefield, NH, 59
Whitman, Walt, 11, 24
Wilson, Edwin, 6, 7, 12, 17, 18, 21, 22, 36, 37, *37*, 46, *47*, *48*, 64, 81, 88-89, 94, 96, *97*, *99*, 104, 107, 113, 114, 123-24, *128*, 136, 147
Wilson, Eddie, 21, 39, 45, 47, 84, 88, 92, 95, 146
Wilson, Julie, 45, 122, 134, 146
Wilson, Sally, 16, 45, 122, 134, 146, 148
Wise, Ray, 129
Woolf, Virginia, 59

Z. Smith Reynolds Foundation, 4, 8, 64, 89
Zuber, Isabel, 59-60, 145, 151

New Hope cemetery
photo by Diane Vitale, 2019

Emily Herring Wilson, a Georgia native, graduated from Woman's College in Greensboro (present-day UNCG), where she studied writing with Randall Jarrell and published poems in the student literary magazine. She spent much of her undergraduate years organizing campus activities, planning celebrations, and loving college. This proved to be the pattern of her life.

After graduation, she enrolled in a master's degree program in English at Wake Forest, and afterwards took a job teaching in the English Department. In 1964 she married the Wake Forest Dean Edwin Wilson, and they built a casual contemporary house in the faculty residential neighborhood. Their three children—Eddie, Sally, and Julie—brought into the family circle Laurie, Carolyn, John, and four grandchildren—Buddy, Harry, Maria, and Ellie, who delight in books, camping, and travel.

Portrait of Emily Herring Wilson
by Ken Bennett

Active in campus and community affairs throughout her many years living in Winston-Salem, Emily became a staunch Democrat, a feminist, and a networker for cultural, racial, and literary lives and public programs. She volunteered in public schools, worked in community colleges as Visiting Artist, wrote for the Winston-Salem Journal, lectured for the North Carolina Humanities Council, and taught at Reynolda House Museum of American Art, Salem College, Wake Forest University, and for a semester at Cornell.

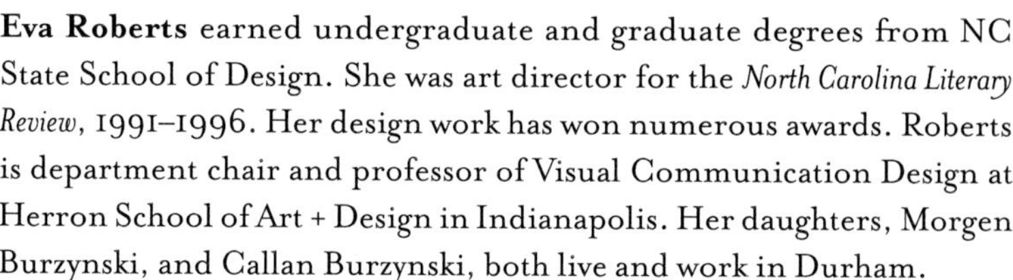

Eva Roberts earned undergraduate and graduate degrees from NC State School of Design. She was art director for the *North Carolina Literary Review*, 1991–1996. Her design work has won numerous awards. Roberts is department chair and professor of Visual Communication Design at Herron School of Art + Design in Indianapolis. Her daughters, Morgen Burzynski, and Callan Burzynski, both live and work in Durham.

Photographers

Susan Mullally is from Oakland. After graduating from the University of California-Berkeley, she earned her MA at UNC-G and MFA at UNC-CH. She taught photography in the Baylor University Art Department and at Christopher Newport University in Williamsburg, VA.

Diane Vitale is a freelance photographer based in Bladenboro, NC, where she also teaches at Bladen Community College.

Jeffrey Cox is the son of Allen Cox, Sr., and Vida Ammons Cox. He lives in Clarkton, NC.